S0-BCP-293

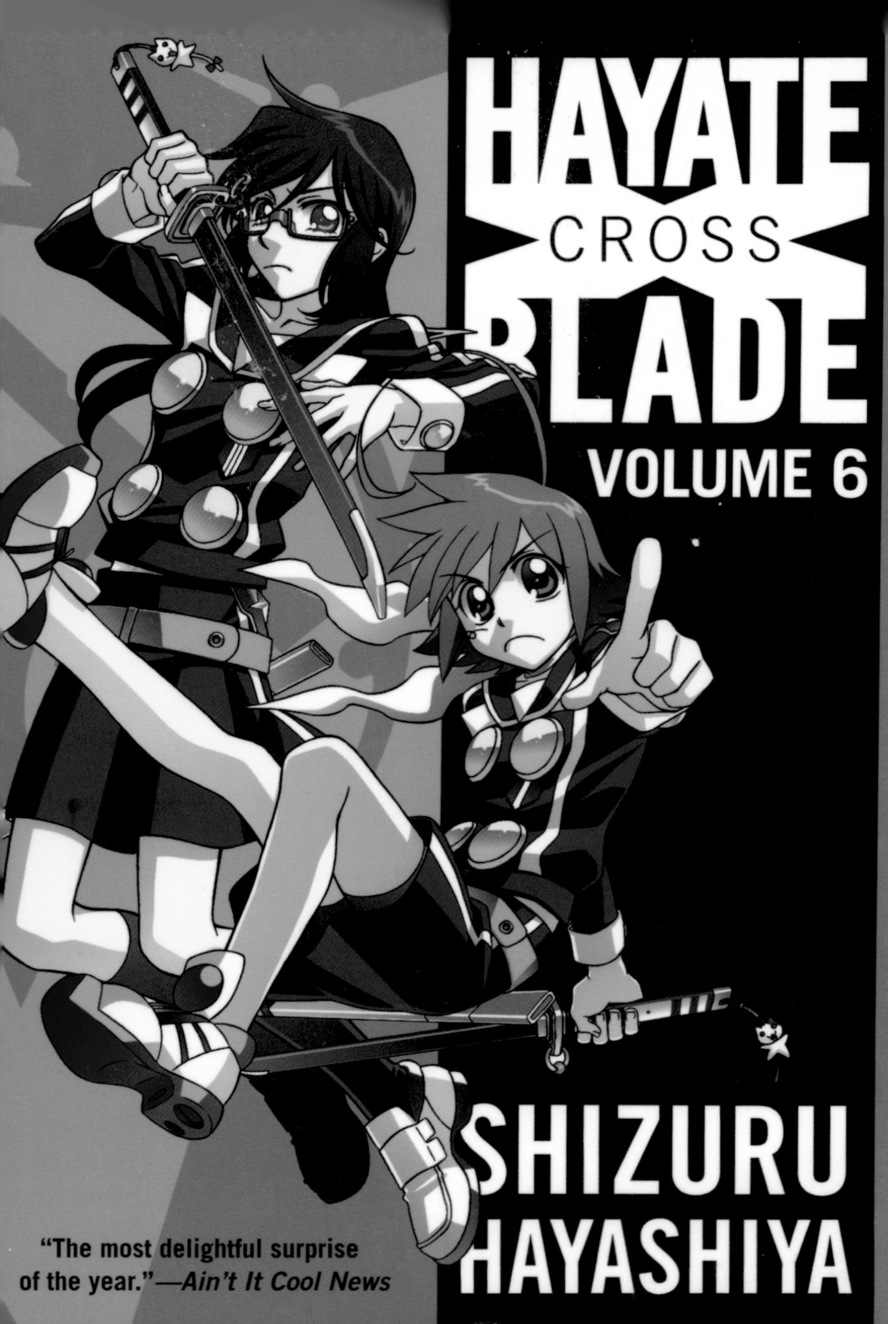
HAYATE
CROSS
BLADE
VOLUME 6
SHIZURU
HAYASHIYA
"The most delightful surprise
of the year."—Ain't It Cool News

A Tor/Seven Seas Book

HAYATE CROSS BLADE 6

SHIZURU HAYASHIYA

HAYATE CROSS BLADE

Volume 6

story & art by Shizuru Hayashiya

STAFF CREDITS

translation Adrienne Beck
adaptation MangaCast, LLC.
cover design Vanessa Paolantonio
lettering & retouch Roland Amago
layout Bambi Eloriaga-Amago
copy editor Erica Friedman
editor Adam Arnold

A Tor/Seven Seas Publication

Visit us online at www.gomanga.com and www.tor-forge.com.

ISBN 978-0-7653-2545-7

TOR®

Printed in the USA

First printing: April 2010

10 9 8 7 6 5 4 3 2 1

CONTENTS

6

#31 Idiot Carnival

I SEE...
THANK YOU FOR THE REPORT. YOU MAY LEAVE NOW.
THAT TEARS IT. THAT LITTLE MIDDLE SCHOOL FIRST YEAR HAS FINALLY CROSSED THE LINE.
I CAN'T BELIEVE HER... BUTT...
HER ASS
SHE RAMMED INTO *OUR ANGEL* WITH HER BEHIND!
OUR DECISION IS UNANIMOUS. SHE IS TO BE *DISPOSED* OF. HOWEVER...
DESPITE BEING A LOWLY FIRST YEAR, SHE IS KNOWN TO BE ONE OF THE MORE DANGEROUS SWORD-BEARERS.
GETTING RID OF HER WILL NOT BE EASY.
WHAT SHALL WE DO?
KIKKAWA-SAMA? HOTEI-SAMA?
THERE SHOULDN'T BE A PROBLEM.

OUR INVES-TIGATION INTO THE BACK-GROUND OF KUROGANE HAYATE...

IS COMPLETE. WE KNOW EVERYTHING WE NEED TO KNOW.

INCLUDING THE FACT THAT ON THE FIRST DAY OF THE SCHOOL FESTIVAL, SHE HAS FAMILY COMING.

ANALYZING PAST DATA, WE KNOW THERE IS ONLY A 20% CHANCE THAT THE BELL WILL TOLL ON THE FIRST DAY OF THE FESTIVAL.

OUR PREFERRED METHOD OF DEALING WITH IMPERTINENT UPSTARTS WITHIN THE RANKS HAS ALWAYS BEEN WITH THE SWORD.

HOW-EVER...
SINCE THIS PARTICULAR TARGET IS IN A LEAGUE SO FAR ABOVE US IT ISN'T EVEN FUNNY...
WE WILL SIMPLY HAVE TO MAKE USE OF THE FIRST DAY OF THE FESTIVAL--WHICH WON'T HAVE A HOSHITORI--TO DO SOMETHING UNDERHANDED.
Ah.
SO WE'RE RESORTING TO DIRTY TRICKS AGAIN, RIGHT?
Perfect.
FASH

#31 Idiot Carnival

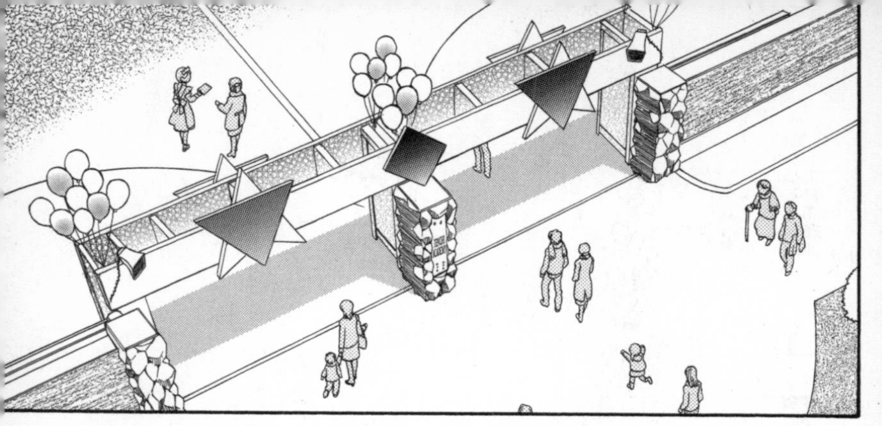

TENCHI ACADEMY SCHOOL FESTIVAL: DAY 1

SOUTH-CENTRAL WING, 3F MAID CAFÉ

YAMMER

YAMMER

YAMMER

YAMMER

COSPLAY PHOTOS

!......

KAICHO ...

YOU REALIZE THIS HARDLY LOOKS ANYTHING LIKE A TYPICAL SCHOOL FESTIVAL.

True, true.

PERHAPS I SHOULD HAVE CALLED THIS YEAR'S EVENT THE TENCHI ACADEMY *AKIHABARA* FESTIVAL.

Hee hee...

SQUEE

I DON'T THINK THE TITLE IS THE PROBLEM, KAICHO.

?
WHAT.
A-AYANA...
W-W-W-W...
W-W-W-W-W-W-W--!
......
GRR
WHOA, HOT!! GO OUTSIDE IN THAT OUTFIT...
ULTRA
MEGA
CUTE!!
AND YOU MIGHT JUST GET ARRESTED!!!
WHAT THE HELL'S THAT SUPPOSED TO MEAN?!!
And you're wearing the same damn thing!!

My, my...
BUT I WAS JUST KINDA SURPRISED, Y'KNOW?
I DIDN'T EXPECT YOU TO PUT THAT ON WITHOUT KICKING UP MORE OF A FIGHT.
DON'T TELL ME YOU SECRETLY LIKE WEARING FRILLY THINGS?
How maidenly!
NOT REALLY ...
FWIF
FWIF
Ah, crap...
YOU LOOK CRIMINALLY HOT IN THAT OUTFIT, THAT'S ALL.
I THINK I MIGHT BE GETTING DIZZY...
I SEE.
YES, YOUR LECHEROUS OGLING CAN DEFINITELY BE CONSIDERED CRIMINAL.
Let's go.
I AVOID THE STUPID FROU-FROU THINGS BECAUSE THEY'RE A PAIN IN THE BUTT TO MOVE AROUND IN.
BUT SINCE WE'RE TAKING THIS HOSHITORI OFF, I WON'T NEED TO WORRY ABOUT THAT.
TCH!
BESIDES, I'M NOT GOING TO GO AGAINST WHAT THE WHOLE CLASS AGREED UPON.
NOT WHEN I SLEPT THROUGH THE VOTE.
WISH I'D KNOWN THAT AHEAD OF TIME. I KNEW I SHOULD'VE SUGGESTED A MINI-SKIRT PUB INSTEAD!
No wait! Panty-less shabu-shabu!!
YOU STILL HAVEN'T LEARNED, HAVE YOU...?
I THINK I JUST DID.
urf...
OW...

W-
W-
W-
WHOA?!!
RENAISSANCE PASSION AYANA~!!!
SHIVER
......
GREAT. MORE IDIOTS.
GREAT WORK!
NICE JOB, JUN-JUN! THIS IS SO GREAT I COULD PEE MYSELF!!
SMACK
AWESOME, HAYATE-CHAN! I KNEW YOU'D UNDER-STAND!
SMACK
YAY!
MUDOU AYANA...
IS THE MAID HOMERUN KING!!
WOOHOO
Sheesh...
GLAD YOU TWO FOUND SOMEONE WHO UNDER-STANDS. BYE.
WAIT, NO! DON'T GO, AYANA!!
I WANNA GET A BETTER LOOK AT ALL YOUR FRILLY BITS!!!
HAAH
HAAH
AUGH!! KEEP YOUR BAD INNUENDO AWAY FROM ME!!!

......
TODAY IS SUPPOSED TO BE THE FIRST DAY OF THE FESTIVAL, RIGHT?
SIGMA !!!
Ah.
SO THE LITTLE DUCKLING IS YOU, SHORTY.
I couldn't tell...
YU...
YUHO...
YUHO!
YUHOOO-OOOON!!!

WAUGH
Anyway...
THIS WASN'T THE REACTION I WAS EXPECTING.
AYANA, DID YOU SHOW HER MY POSTCARD?
WELCOME HOME, HIME-SAMA...
IT HAS BEEN FAR TOO LONG.
I'M NOT HOME YET. AND IT'S BARELY BEEN A MONTH SINCE I LEFT.
AND you visited me not that long ago.
ER... SORRY 'BOUT THAT.
I KINDA HAD TO STOP A CERTAIN DEMON FROM GOING ON A RAMPAGE.
I SEE.
IT'S ALL RIGHT. I UNDERSTAND.
I'll ask for the details... LATER.
I'M SURE IT'S ENTIRELY THE DEMON'S FAULT. SHE'S DENSE LIKE THAT.
......

BEEN LOOKIN' ALL OVER FOR YOU!
HFF
HFF
HFF
AH.
MOKA-CHAN.
MOMO-CHI...?
WOW. THAT'S, UH... *QUITE* THE LOOK FOR YOU.
WHAT, THIS?
SQUEEK
YOU'VE GOTTA GET ON BACK TO THE BOOTH, QUICK!
SQUEEK
SQUEEK
WELL, YEAH! EVERYBODY KNOWS THE DUCKY'S BEST PAL IS A MOUSE!!
I PICKED IT ALL BY MYSELF, TOO!
HEH HEH!
OH...
GAVE UP.
WAIT. OH YEAH!
KUROGANE! I WAS LOOKIN' FOR YOU.
HUH?
Need more help?
ALL THE DANDELION GARDEN KIDS ARE HERE! YOU GOTTA GET BACK TO THE STAND!!
DON'T WANNA LEAVE THEM HANGIN' OUT TO DRY, NOW DO YA?
WHA?! THEY'RE HERE ALREADY ?!!

OH MY GOSH! AYANA, WE HAVE TO HURRY!!
WE HAFTA GET TO THE SCENE RIGHT NOW!!!
FLUTTER
FLUTTER
FLUTTER
WAIT, HOLD ON!
WHY DO I NEED TO GO?!
BECAUSE I PROMISED EVERYBODY WE'D TAKE THEM AROUND THE FESTIVAL TOGETHER!!
NOW HURRY UP AND PUT THIS ON!!!
RSTL
?
O-OKAY...!
FLUTTER
HUH ?!
FLUTTER
LAWSON
GREAT !!
RUSTLE
LAWSON MAID MASK TRANS-FORM!
TA-DAH!! FAMILY MART DUCK-- ...WHA?!!
MY MASK!
MY HEAD WON'T FIT IN MY MASK?!!
HUPH
HOW ABOUT YOU COOL DOWN AND START USING THAT BRAIN OF YOURS, NITWIT!!
Is THIS really necessary?!
ACTUALLY, WHY DON'T THE TWO OF YOU JUST GO?
NOW IT'S MY TURN!
FWUF
ふもー

GOD ...!
GUESS I'D BETTER. SORRY, JUN! KEEP AN EYE ON THINGS FOR ME!
I SHOULDN'T BE LONG!
I think it'll be okay. We've got plenty of maids.
YEAH, SURE. WHATEVER. HAVE FUN!
HUNH ...
I GUESS EVEN RAGING TIGER AYANA CAN'T ABANDON THE LITTLE GUESTS.
THAT'S GOOD.
What a nice big sister.
IS IT ME, OR IS AYANA... DIFFERENT?
HM?
SHE SEEMS, I DON'T KNOW... SOFTER AROUND THE EDGES.
MAYBE IT'S BECAUSE OF THE OUTFIT.
YOU'VE GOT A POINT.
I GUESS YOU'RE PROBABLY RIGHT.
BET IT'S ALL THANKS TO HAYATE-CHAN.
IT SURE DOESN'T LOOK IT, BUT SHE'S GOT SOME PRETTY INCREDIBLE POWERS WHEN IT COMES TO PEOPLE.

THE SCHOOL FESTIVAL'S ALWAYS BEEN ROYALLY DULL BEFORE...
BUT THIS YEAR'S LOOKS LIKE IT'S GOING TO BE FUN!
Ah.
OH!
BY THE WAY, DID AYANA'S PARENTS COME?
NOPE.
DIDN'T COME LAST YEAR, EITHER.
AYANA'S GOT SOME FAMILY ISSUES TOO, I GUESS.
SOMEYA'S THE ONLY ONE WHO'D KNOW THE DETAILS.
HAYATE!
MAKES WHAT HAYATE-CHAN DOES ALL THE GREATER, REALLY.
SHE TAKES ALL THAT AND HELPS MAKE THE LOAD LIGHTER ON AYANA.
......
YEAH ...
ANY-WAY.
WHAT ABOUT YOU? DID YOUR MOTHER COME WITH YOU?
NO.
MOM SAID SHE HAD AN APPOINTMENT, SO SHE SENT UNCLE KUGA WITH ME...
DAD'S HERE?!
WAS. THE MAIDS MADE HIS HEAD HURT, SO HE LEFT.
He should be back later, though.
UH...

EVERYBODY READY FOR THE TENCHI ACADEMY GRAND TOUR, OVER HERE!!
OKAY!!
YAAAAY!!!
I'M SO SORRY TO PUT YOU THROUGH ALL THIS TROUBLE, AYANA-CHAN.
I'M SURE YOU HAD OTHER THINGS YOU NEEDED TO DO FOR YOUR OWN CLASS, AS WELL.
Meganee-chan!
IT'S OKAY!
IN FOR A PENNY, IN FOR A POUND AND ALL THAT...
Meganee-chan!
OH, YOU ARE SUCH A SWEET CHILD!
FOR SOMEONE AS WONDERFUL AND KIND AS YOU, AYANA-CHAN...
I WILL GLADLY *ALLOW* YOU TO *HAVE* HAYATE-CHAN!
THEN, ONCE YOU HAVE FINISHED SCHOOL, *BOTH OF YOU* WILL COME AND BE MY WIVES!
SEEING YOU TODAY, IN THIS OUTFIT, WAS EXACTLY WHAT I WISHED FROM THE BOTTOM OF MY HEART!
I'll be waiting!
HUH?
UH, WAIT A MINUTE... WHOA. HOLD ON.
WHAT ARE YOU TALKING ABOUT?
HN...?
GLANCE
HUH...?

COTTON CANDY
Cutie Pure
CAT
CHIHARU-SAAAN.
YES?
WHERE'S MIKI? I DON'T SEE HER.
OH MY...
THAT'S ODD. SHE WAS HERE JUST A MOMENT AGO.
HM. MAYBE SHE WENT TO THE POTTY.
ARE YOU SURE THAT'S OKAY?
I MEAN, SOME WEIRDO COULD'VE MADE OFF WITH HER, Y'KNOW.
After all, this campus is full of nothing but weirdos...
NAH! SHE'S FINE!
MIKI'S EVEN SMARTER THAN ME!
FOR A YOUNG CHILD TO WANDER THESE GROUNDS ALONE...
IS FAR MORE DANGEROUS THAN SIMPLE KIDNAPPING!
LOOOOM

......
O-OH... IT'S YOU, INU-CHAN.
I THOUGHT FOR A SECOND SOME VOODOO-DOLL HAD COME TO LIFE...
BDMP
BDMP
BDMP
REALLY ...?
Y-YOU FLATTER ME.
Uh, that wasn't a compliment...
YEESH. SHE'S NOT SO MUCH A MAID AS AN EXTRA-FRILLY GRAVE GUARDIAN.
WAIT--!
IT IS TOO DANGEROUS FOR A CHILD TO WANDER THESE GROUNDS! THEY'RE TOO HUGE!
AND THERE ARE TOO MANY DANGEROUS "ZONES" A CHILD WITHOUT THE PROPER SENSES COULD BECOME LOST IN!
YES...
ZONES OF NEGATIVE ENERGY.
PUT SIMPLY, THEY ARE PLACES A CHILD MAY BE SPIRITED AWAY--THE KAMIKAKUSHI ZONES!
THESE PLACES MAY BE HARMLESS TO US, BUT TO A CHILD...
SPIRITED AWAY...
......
JUST WHAT PLANE OF EXISTENCE IS OUR WORLD SUPPOSED TO BELONG TO, HUH?
ZONES ?
?
I'D LISTEN TO HER, KUROGANE. IF WANKO SAYS IT'S DANGEROUS, THEN IT PROLLY IS.
She's good at that kinda stuff.
I'D THINK GOING TO LOOK FOR THE KID WOULD BE A GOOD IDEA.
URK.
Yeah, maybe...

IT APPEARS ...
THAT YOU MAY HAVE NEED OF MY TALENTS.
AH!
LOSER KIJI!
QUIT IT WITH THE "LOSER" BIT!
DESPITE THAT, I'M NOT AVERSE TO GIVING YOU ALL A HELPING HAND.
FINDING LOST THINGS IS A SPECIALTY OF MINE, AFTER ALL!
WITH THESE SPECIAL DOWSING RO--
GYAAAA!!!
GRIK
M-m-m-
MICHI!!
WHAT DID YOU DO THAT FOR?!
SHING
YOU KNOW THAT IF THE ROD GETS STRAIGHTENED OUT IT CAN'T BE USED ANYMORE!
NO WEIRD GADGETS!
THINGS'LL GET WAY TOO WEIRD AND COMPLICATED IF YOU USE THOSE.
And I just bought them, too...
WE'RE ON BREAK, SO WE'LL HELP YOU LOOK, IF YOU'D LIKE.
I SHALL RETURN TO MY ROOM TO CONSULT MY CRYSTAL BALL...
Thanks!
UNLIKE SOME THINGS, THAT SOUNDS TRUSTWORTHY! WOULD YOU, PLEASE?

O-OKAY...
What, me too?
RIGHT!
LET'S GO, AYANA!
CHIHARU-SAN, WAIT RIGHT THERE. WE'LL FIND HER!
Yeesh!
SILLY MIKI!
Making everybody worry...
TROMP
TROMP
I REALLY APPRECIATE YOU DOING ALL THIS FOR ME, AYANA-CHAN!
And for all the other kids, too, of course.
WHEN YOU COME BACK, I'LL GIVE YOU A BIG HUG!
UH, NO. PLEASE DON'T.
...!
MAYBE THIS...
IS WHAT EVERYBODY MEANS...
WHEN THEY TALK ABOUT...
A NORMAL FAMILY.

BING BOONG
ON AIR!
RIGHT, ATTENTION FESTIVAL GUESTS!
SORRY TO INTERRUPT THE SONG, BUT WE HAVE A CALL OUT FOR A MISSING CHILD.
LET'S SEE...
Wow! This was actually a really great idea coming from you, Kiji-chan!
What do you mean "coming from me"?
MIKI-CHAN! DANDELION GARDEN'S MIKI-CHAN! EVERYONE IS LOOKING FOR YOU, HONEY.
PLEASE GO STRAIGHT TO "MASCOT-LAND SHIGERU," OKAY?
HMM... AYANA AND THEM ARE PROBABLY OUT LOOKING FOR HER.
I HOPE THEY FIND HER SOON.
HN?
SOUNDS LIKE THAT KID IS FROM HAYATE-CHAN'S PLACE.
THEY SAID SHE WAS LOST. I HOPE SHE'S OKAY.
HEY, HOW'S ABOUT YOU GO HELP THEM...
SOMEYA?
NO, HOW ABOUT YOU GO AND HELP THEM SEARCH!

WOW, IS THAT THE ATTITUDE YOU USE FOR YOUR CUSTOMERS?
I'D STAY AWAY FROM SERVICE JOBS THEN, IF I WERE YOU.
Booo!
A DEVIL VOYEUR DRESSED IN MAID'S CLOTHING DOES NOT COUNT AS A "CUSTOMER."
...
I TREAT *REAL* GUESTS PROPERLY.
......
So, uh, what?
Does everybody think I'm devil-spawn, now?
SUCCUBUS
VOYEUR
DEMON
I'M SO SORRY TO HAVE KEPT YOU WAITING, MISS.
IT'S WONDERFUL TO SEE YOU LOOKING WELL.
Oh.
THANKS.
THOUGH, I MUST APOLOGIZE.
I SUSPECT JUN MUST HAVE DRAGGED YOU HERE.
SIGH
I'm sure.
SO, DID SHE SAY SHE WAS GOING TO SHOW YOU SOMETHING "INTERESTING"?
AH, NO.
SHE DIDN'T DRAG ME AT ALL.
I TOLD HER THAT I WANTED TO COME SEE YOU.
OH?
YEAH. I DIDN'T HAVE A CHANCE TO MAKE MY PROPER FAREWELLS TO YOU WHEN I MOVED OUT OF THE DORM.
YEP!
WE WERE TALKING ABOUT AYANA AND HER FAMILY AND THAT REMINDED US OF YOU.
SO WE DECIDED TO PASS ON BY AND SAY HI.

WE JUST WANTED TO TALK.

YEAH.

AND ONE OTHER THING, TOO.

IN THE NEXT HOSHI-TORI...

GO

WIN!

ZWISH

!...

MY...

YOU CAME ALL THE WAY HERE JUST TO TELL ME THAT?

I'M NO FOOL TO GO CHALLENGING SOMEONE I KNOW I CANNOT BEAT.
SO YOU NEEDN'T FUSS.
HEY!
THIS IS SUPPOSED TO BE THE PART WHERE YOU SHOWER US WITH THANKS FOR OUR CONCERN!
THANK YOU, YUHO.
I HOPE TO SEE YOU BACK HERE SOON.
THOUGH, I'M AFRAID I'M TOO BUSY TO BE ABLE TO VISIT YOU IN THE HOSPITAL.
STILL.
IT'S SUCH A SHAME THERE'S ALMOST NO CHANCE THE BELL'S GOING TO RING TODAY.
Drat!
AWWW
WE WERE SO LOOKING FORWARD TO WATCHING YOU FIGHT, YOUR LOVELY DRESS FLARING AROUND YOU TO SHOW OFF TANTALIZING PANTY-FLASHES.
What do you mean "we"?
I WILL NOT BE FLASHING ANY-THING!!!
I DON'T REALLY WANT TO SEE THAT, EITHER...

NNN
N...
THIS IS SO WEIRD...!
WHERE COULD MIKI BE?!
Her hiney's gonna get a spankin' now!
STICKING TOGETHER MEANS WE CAN'T COVER AS MUCH GROUND.
LET'S SPLIT UP AND LOOK AGAIN.
RIGHT!
I'LL TAKE THE CLASSROOM BUILDINGS. YOU CHECK OUT AROUND THE BOOTHS.
WE'VE GOTTEN PRETTY FAR AWAY FROM THE MAIN FESTIVAL GROUNDS, TOO.
SOMETHING'S DEFINITELY WRONG HERE. WE SHOULD'VE FOUND HER BY NOW.
MIIIIKI!
WHERE ARE YA?!
RSTL
......

THE TARGET HAS BEGUN SOLO MOVEMENT. REPEAT, THE TARGET IS SOLO.
IT'S ABOUT TIME.
SNAP
SORRY. BUT DON'T WORRY, IT WON'T BE TOO MUCH LONGER NOW...
MESSAGE DELIVERY IS GO.
PEE-WEE-SAN.
TA—DAAA
M'KAY.
ROGER. MESSENGER WILL BE INFORMED.
I'LL BE GOOD FOR 10 CHIRORI CHOCO-LATES.
CRISPY!
YUMMY!
CHOCOLATE REVIENNE EPISODE I
HNNN...
YAMMER
YAMMER
THIS HUGE CROWD MAKES IT SO HARD TO SPOT ANYBODY...

CRAP.
NOW I'M REALLY STARTING TO GET WORRIED.
I HOPE SHE DIDN'T REALLY GET CAUGHT IN A SPIRIT-KUSHI HOLE OR SOME-THING.
HYAAAA —— !!!
THAT'S TOO SCARY TO THINK ABOUT!!
I GOTTA FIND HER FAST!!
WH-WHAT IF, BY THE TIME WE FIND HER...
Hayate, I'm baaack!
SHE'S IN THE BODY OF A FULL GROWN, MATURE WOMAN?!
BDMP
BDMP
BDMP
TWITCH
びくっ
THWOK
HYAAAAA —— ?!!
......?
WHAT'S THIS...?
#31 END

W/h-what if, by the time we find her, she's already a dynamite sexy woman...?!

Hayate~!

BIG BOOBS

TINY WAIST

NICE BUTT

I think in this case, the first thing we should do is get you away from Jun.

TENCHI ACADEMY  SWORD-BEARER LIST

■増田 恵 (Masuda Kei)■

Junior High, Class 3-B
Height: 157cm (5'1")
Weight: 46kg (101lbs.)
Birth Date: Jan. 17
Zodiac: Capricorn
Blood Type: O

Junior High, Class 3-E
Height: 156cm (5'1")
Weight: 46kg (101lbs.)
Birth Date: May 9
Zodiac: Taurus
Blood Type: AB

■根本美鶴代 (Nemoto Mitsuyo)■

●FILE EX.●

SHEESH...!
PEOPLE NEED TO BE MORE CAREFUL WITH THESE THINGS!
I ALMOST GOT STUCK IN THE BUTT!
HUH?
#32 Idiot Festival
OH, HEY! THERE'S SOME-THING TIED ON HERE!
MAYBE IT'S A NOTE?
HUP!
OKAY.
LET'S GET IT OFF...
PLOP
HRMPH?
RUFL
HNGH!
......
RUFL
NPH!
WRIGGLE
C'MON... RMPH!
WRIGGLE
IT'S NOT COMIN' OFF!!!
HUFF
HUFF
HERE, LET ME SEE IT.
HUFF
HUFF

THANKS, MISTER!

Uh, you're welcome...

IT LOOKS LIKE IT'S FOR ME.

WHOA...

Tenchi Academy Middle School, Class 1-C
Kurogane Hayate-dono

WARNING

We have taken custody of a young lady known to be a member of your honorable family. If you wish to see her returned to you unharmed, you will promptly come alone to the clock tower located in Northern Court.

-Best,
A-TEAM

LESSEE ...

WHAT——?!!

......

#32 Idiot Festival

IT'S FULL OF WORDS I CAN'T READ!!!
GYAAAAAA
LET ME SEE IT...

RATTLE
RATTLE
HMMM...
GA-CHUNK
THE DOOR...
IS LOCKED!!
THEN THAT MEANS...
CAT-TIVE!
THE EVIL BAD GUYS ARE HOLDIN' THE BEAUTIFUL PRINCESS CATTIVE!
CORRECTION: "CAPTIVE"
TOMATOES
SO...
THAT MEANS...
HAYATE'S GONNA COME RESCUE ME!!
SO ALL I HAVE TO DO IS STAY PUT AND EAT CANDY!
Yeah!
DILEMMA SOLVED.
MR. POTATO

COULD SHE BE IN HERE...?
SWF
NOPE. NOT HERE.
Thought not.
Maid Cafe KOMACHI
YEAH, A KID ISN'T GOING TO HANG AROUND IN A TEA HOUSE BY HERSELF.
Hmm...
MORE LIKELY SHE'S IN THE EXHIBIT HALL OR THE AUDITORIUM.
MUDOU-SAN?
I HAD WONDERED WHAT SHAMELESS OUTFIT YOU MIGHT BE WEARING, BUT IT'S ACTUALLY QUITE NORMAL.
HOW SURPRISING.
This is my classroom.
ARE YOU SEARCHING FOR SOMEONE?
HUH?
......!
OH! UH...?
STOP. IT'S OKAY. YOU NEEDN'T FORCE YOURSELF TO RECALL MY NAME.
WAP

OH. ER, WELL...
YEAH, I'M LOOKING FOR SOMEONE.
A LITTLE HUMAN.
ABOUT, SAY... THIS BIG?
...
IF YOU MEAN "CHILD" THEN JUST SAY "CHILD"!
Don't beat around the bush!
I ASSUME YOU MEAN THE GIRL MEN-TIONED OVER THE INTER-COM?
SHE'S ONE OF THE CHILDREN FROM KUROGANE-SAN'S ORPHANAGE, YES? SORRY, I HAVE NOT SEEN CHILDREN SO FAR.
AH. OKAY.
I'LL TAKE A LOOK AROUND ELSE-WHERE, THEN.
LATER.
YOU'RE WEL-COME.
OH, MUDOU-SAN?
WOULD YOU TELL ME WHAT THE CHILD LOOKS LIKE?
SOU AND MYSELF WILL BE GOING ON BREAK SHORTLY. WE CAN HELP WITH THE SEARCH THEN.

WHAT SHE LOOKS LIKE?
Ummm...
SHORT. KINDA BLACK-ISH AT THE TOP...
JUST TELL ME WHAT COLOR CLOTHES SHE IS WEARING!
Sheesh!
What on earth are you looking for?!
OH, UH, LIGHT-BLUE. I THINK.
Light blue hoodie, maybe...?
ANYWAY, THAT'S PRETTY MUCH WHAT SHE LOOKS LIKE!
THANKS A LOT...
ASAKURA-SAN!
2F
AH...
WAIT, NO.
SASA-KUMA-SAN...
NO, THAT'S NOT RIGHT EITHER.
AH WELL. THANKS, OKAMI-SAN!!
Anyways, it's appreciated.
BLAM

MIZUCHI-SAN!
I'M SO SORRY I'M LATE. I--
YIKES!!
SHE'S *ALREADY* DEPRESSED?!!
But strangely attractive all the same...!
SOU...
VICTORY IS A FICKLE LADY...
FOR AN INSTANT YOU THINK YOU HAVE FINALLY GRASPED IT... ONLY TO FIND IT HAS VANISHED FROM YOUR HAND LIKE MIST...
ALL THAT REMAINS... IS OKAMI-SAN...
WHA...?
A BREAK! FORGET WHAT HAPPENED. YOU NEED TO TAKE A BREAK, MIZUCHI-SAN!!
......
WOULD YOU KNOCK IT OFF ALREADY?!
STOP SQUIRMING AROUND!
GAWD!

SERIOUSLY, AKIRA.
IT'S NOT EVERY DAY THAT I DECIDE TO GIVE SOMEONE MY SPECIAL GLAMOUR MANICURE, SO HOLD STILL!
Now I have to start all over AGAIN!
I WOULD IF YOU'D STOP TAKING FREAKIN' FOREVER! SPEED IT UP A LITTLE!!
OH, COME ON, AKIRA.
THIS IS YOUR OWN FAULT, YOU KNOW. YOU WERE THE ONE WHO DECIDED HALF-JOKINGLY TO DEMAND KUREA BE THE ONE TO DO YOUR NAILS.
OH, DON'T GET SO UPSET. I JUST WANT TO HELP YOU LOOK LOVELY, THAT'S ALL.
YEAH, SHE, LIKE, REALLY COULD STAND TO LOOK A LITTLE PRETTIER AROUND THE EDGES.
You so need to learn how to trim your nails properly.
DAMMIT!!
What do you think?
Sigh
HEY, HOW ABOUT YOU STOP WORRYING ABOUT ME AND PRETTY HER UP FIRST?
YOU KNOW, THAT DROOLING PUPPY THAT ALWAYS FOLLOWS YOU AROUND EVERYWHERE?
......
IMPOSSIBLE. SHE TRIES TO LICK HER FINGERS RIGHT AFTER I FINISH HER NAILS.
LIAR!! YOU WERE THE ONE WHO TOLD KUREA TO DO IT OR ELSE!!!
Oh! SPEAKING OF MINORI, I HAVEN'T SEEN HER AROUND.
SHE'S LIKELY OFF BY THE FOOD BOOTHS, STUFFING HER FACE.

WHATEVER. SERIOUSLY, WOULD YOU HURRY UP AND FINISH THIS?
We've already been too long...
IT'S NOT LIKE WE'VE GOT ALL DAY TO KILL, HERE. WE'VE GOT TO GET BACK TO OUR PATROL ROUNDS, AND WE BOTH HAVE RESPONSIBILITIES BACK AT OUR OWN BOOTHS AS WELL.
ば
FWUP
PARDON ME!
さっ
YEAH! IT'S LIKE PARDON THE WAIT--
HUH?
NOPE.
Not here, either.
SORRY!
DMP
......
Hey...
SAE...
THAT WAS THE STUPID SQUIRT'S PARTNER, RIGHT?
AUGH! How many times do I have to tell you, hold still!!
YES, IT WAS. IT LOOKED LIKE SHE WAS SEARCHING FOR SOMEONE.
TMPA
TMPA
TMPA
TMPA
KUROGANE-SAN, PERHAPS?
......

ALL RIGHT.
C'MON, SAE. LET'S GO.
TNK
HEY!
WAIT A MINUTE! I'M NOT DONE YET!!
MY NAILS ALREADY LOOK GREAT, THOUGH.
NOT LIKE YOU'D EVER DO LESS THAN PERFECTION, KUREA.
THANKS.
B-BUT...
I, LIKE, ONLY FILED THEM AND PAINTED ON THE BASE COAT!
COME BACK AND LET ME FINISH, DAMMIT!!
YOU CAN FINISH THEM LATER.
I'VE GOT A HUNCH SOMETHING'S UP, AND WE'D BETTER FIND OUT WHAT.
You know, you're right.
YOU CAN'T FOOL ME!
I KNOW WHAT'S UP. YOU TOTALLY CAME HERE JUST TO BLOW OFF WORK!
No, no.
NOT TRUE.
WE STOPPED BY TO VISIT AND PLAY *WITH* YOU.
GRAAAH!
WHAT'S WITH THAT "WITH"?!

CHUNK
HNNN ...
NAAAH ...
OF COURSE SHE'S NOT GOING TO BE IN THERE.
BURNABLE TRASH
SIGH
CRAP.
SO THE ONLY PLACES LEFT TO LOOK ARE--
MUDOU-SAAANNNNNNN !!!!
WAAAA-AAAAAH ?!!

THE...
C-CAN'T YOU JUST WALK UP AND SAY "HEY" LIKE, Y'KNOW, NORMAL PEOPLE...?
BURNABLE TRASH
I- I-
INU-GIRL...?
THE PORTENTS!
MUDOU-SAN, THE PORTENTS ARE TERRIBLE...!
!
YOU FOUND THE KID? IS SOMETHING WRONG?!
NO... I-I HAVE AN IDEA WHERE SHE IS...
AND THE SIGNS SAY THAT SHE IS UNHARMED...
BUT WHAT MY CRYSTAL HAS SHOWN TO ME IS THE INSIDE OF A STOREROOM.
I ASSUME IT IS ONE OF THE MANY HERE ON CAMPUS, BUT WHICH ONE IS UNCLEAR.
B-BUT THAT IS NOT THE TERRIFYING PART...
SHE IS LOCKED INSIDE THAT STOREROOM, MUDOU-SAN. LOCKED IN!
THAT MEANS...
THIS... THIS ALL IS...
....

WHAT ABOUT KURO?
HAVE YOU TOLD HER YET?
AH!
TH-THAT IS EVEN WORSE!
I COMMANDED MY CRYSTAL BALL TO SHOW ME HER LOCATION SO THAT I COULD TELL HER THE NEWS.
BUT WHAT I FOUND...
WAS KUROGANE-SAN ALONE, SURROUNDED BY DOZENS AND DOZENS OF STUDENTS ALL HUNGERING FOR HER BLOOD!
WH- WHAT IS GOING ON?!
WHA ?!
GOD, WHAT DOES THAT FLUFF-BRAINED LITTLE DUNCE THINK SHE'S DOING?!
......
IN ANY CASE, BETTER GO FIND THE USELESS RUNT. I'M BETTING WHATEVER SHE'S GOTTEN HERSELF INTO...
HAS GOT SOMETHING TO DO WITH WHY THE KID'S LOCKED UP.
O- OKAY.
THE SIGNS POINT TO HER BEING BY THE CLOCK TOWER IN THE NORTH COURT...
THANKS! TAKE CARE OF WHATEVER ELSE YOU CAN, OKAY?

……
WELCOME, KUROGANE-SAN.
I SEE YOU FOLLOWED OUR INSTRUCTIONS AND CAME ALONE. VERY BRAVE OF YOU.
UH, THAT'S COOL AN' ALL...
BUT CAN I ASK A QUES-TION?
WHY'S EVERYBODY IN THE FRONT ROW WEARING GLASSES?
I'D RATHER NOT EXPLAIN. IT'S A LONG STORY.

SO WHERE'S MIKI? HAND HER OVER!!
OH. OKAY. NEVERMIND THEN.
MI~KI MI~KI!!
YOU KNOW, GETTING BRUSHED OFF LIKE THAT IS REALLY MAKING ME WANT TO EXPLAIN IT NOW.
ANY-WAY...
DON'T WORRY ABOUT THE GIRL. SHE IS BEING WELL TAKEN CARE OF.
HOWEVER, THAT CAN ALL CHANGE VERY DRASTICALLY DEPENDING UPON YOUR RESPONSE.
GIMME MIKI ALREADY!!!
I HAVEN'T GIVEN HER MY GRAND TOUR OF THE ACADEMY YET!
MI~KI~!!
DWAH!
MI~KI~!!
H-HEY!
MI~KI~!!
LISTEN TO WHAT WE HAVE TO SAY FIRST!! AND GET OFF OF ME!!!
ばららららっ
FWAAAAAP
TENCHI ACADEMY MIDDLE SCHOOL, CLASS 1-C, KUROGANE HAYATE!!
THE FOLLOWING...
GET OFFA ME!!
HUH?
IS AN ACCOUNT OF YOUR CRIMES AND SINS!!!

NAMELY!!!
MULTIPLE COUNTS OF IMPOLITENESS, IMPROPRIETY AND GENERAL FAMILIARITY...
WITH SHE WHO IS OUR ANGEL, OUR IDOL, OUR UNAPPROACHABLE AND UNASSAIL-ABLE GODDESS: S RANK SWORD BEARER MIKADO AKIRA!!!
MOREOVER, YOUR MOST VILE OFFENSE, IN WHICH YOU CRASHED INTO HER AUGUST PERSON WITH YOUR BUTTOCKS, FLAGRANTLY TRAMPLE UPON HER DIGNITY IN A MOST UNFORGIVABLE MANNER!!
?
ACCORDINGLY, WE 80 MEMBERS OF THE MIKADO AKIRA FAN CLUB--ALTERNATELY KNOWN AS THE A(KIRA) TEAM--DO UNANIMOUSLY FIND YOU GUILTY OF GROSS MISCONDUCT!
WE HEREBY DEMAND THE MAXIMUM PUNISHMENT FOR YOU, THE ACCUSED, KUROGANE HAYATE!!!

SO...
DO YOU UNDER-STAND EVERYTHING SO FAR?
Yeee!!
HFF
HFF
HFF
HFF
UMM...
NOPE! DIDN'T GET MOST OF IT...
BUT I DID HEAR MIKADON, BUTTS AND NIPPLE.
WHAT ABOUT 'EM?
"TRAMPLE"!! I SAID "TRAMPLE" YOU INTOLERABLE IDIOT!!!
DO YOU HAVE ANY IDEA HOW MANY MENTAL IMAGES THAT JUST PROMPTED?!
BLUUUSH
WHAT DO YOU THINK WE ARE, JUNIOR HIGH BOYS?!!
THAT DOES IT!!
ENOUGH!! LET ME PUT IT BLUNTLY ENOUGH FOR YOU TO UNDERSTAND!!
YOU BUG US, SO WE WANT YOU OUT OF THE ACADEMY!!!
POINT
WHAP
WHAAAAAAT?!!!
Why?!

DA-DAAN
WHAT?!
WANKO, THAT FOR REAL?!!
Um...
Y-YES.
KUROGANE-SAN IS FACING A LARGE NUMBER OF OPPONENTS BY HERSELF...
THOUGH MUDOU-SAN IS ON HER WAY THERE AS WE SPEAK.
A BRAWL!
Okay.
TP
TP
TP
UM... MOMOKA-SAN?
YOU SEEM AWFULLY HAPPY ABOUT THIS...
TP
TP
'COURSE I AM! BRAWLS ARE THE BEST PART OF A FESTIVAL!
DON'T KNOW EXACTLY WHAT'S GOIN' ON, BUT SINCE IT'S A WHOLE BUNCH OF THEM VERSUS KUROGANE, I'M THINKIN' SHE GOT CALLED OUT.
Looks like she did somethin' dumb again...
AN' THAT MEANS THE MISSING KID'S PROBABLY THEIR HOSTAGE.
C'MON, WANKO! WE'RE HEADIN' OVER THERE RIGHT NOW!!
BUT THAT'S NOT THE POINT. WHAT MATTERS IS THERE'S GONNA BE A FRACAS WHERE WE'LL BE TOTALLY OUTNUMBERED WITH ALMOST NO CHANCE TO WIN.
HEH
HEH
YOU COULDN'T KEEP ME AWAY FROM THIS ONE IF YOU TRIED!
Oh, okay.
NOW I KNOW ONE MORE THING THAT MAKES YOU HAPPY, MOMOKA-SAN!

GOD...
A *PROPER* SWORD-BEARER SHOULDN'T LET HERSELF GET CARRIED AWAY SO EASILY.
YOU LOOK BARBARIC INSTEAD OF DAPPER.
GYA!!
Kiji!
STOP BUBBLIN' UP FROM OUT OF NOWHERE ALREADY!!
I've been here the whole time.
YOU STOP BEING TOO BLIND TO NOTICE THE OBVIOUS.
LIKE THE LITTLE FACT THAT YOU'RE GOING TO NEED MORE HELP WITH THIS.
BESIDES...
I'M FOND OF THOSE SCENARIOS MYSELF.
SPARKLE SPARKLE
YOUR FRIENDS ARE SURROUNDED BY ENEMIES, FIGHTING A HOPELESS BATTLE WHEN SUDDENLY--
WHEN SUDDENLY THE HERO APPEARS...
SHOUTING ***"WAIT!"*** AS THE SPOTLIGHT ZOOMS IN ON THEM.
WAIT!
Who is it?
Who's that?
......
JUST SO'S YOU KNOW... *I* GET THAT PART.

HN?
CHEMISTRY CLUB
3F
Maid Karaoke
Hey.
THERE'S MOMO-CHI.
Gah, those two are too fast!
GYAAA
GYAAA
WONDER WHERE THEY'RE OFF TO, BLOOD-LUST AND ALL...
JUN, DON'T YOU THINK THERE'S SOMETHING ODD GOING ON?
HN?
EVERY ONE OF THEM...
AAH.
YOU'RE RIGHT.
Hunh.
LOOK AT THEM.
IS CARRYING THEIR SWORD.
Wonder why that is.
WHY WOULD THEY BE DOING THAT WHEN IT'S ALMOST CERTAIN THE BELL WON'T RING TODAY?

THAT'S WHAT I WANT TO KNOW.
GO FIND OUT.
HUH ?!
WHA, ME? WHY NOW?!
YOU PROBABLY WANT TO KNOW WHAT'S GOING ON EVEN MORE THAN I DO, RIGHT?
SO GO ON. GO.
Besides, I want to go visit Kei-chan.
......
YOU'RE ABSOLUTELY CORRECT, HIME...
AH!
BUT DON'T GO LEAVING ON ME WHILE I'M GONE, GOT IT?
I HAVEN'T HAD A CHANCE TO SEE DAD YET, EITHER!
DUH. OF COURSE I WON'T. I WAS PLANNING ON FOLLOWING AFTER YOU LATER ANYWAY.
OKAY!
IF THAT'S THE CASE, I'LL SEE YOU LATER!
FWISH
MISS YUHO...
So here you are.
Ah.
UNCLE.
Oh dear. You just missed her.
ARE YOU FEELING BETTER?
SORT OF...
Y'SEE, I WAS RESTING WHEN THIS...
DUCK WITH AN ARROW CAME, AND--
?

AH!
WELL, THE KID'S SAFE, SO THAT'S GOOD 'N ALL...
BUT WE ALSO FOUND OUT THAT KUROGANE'S GOTTEN HERSELF INTO A PRETTY BIG FIX.
What?
REALLY?! WHAT HAPPENED?
MOMOKA-CHAN!
SORRY! DON'T GOT THE TIME TO EXPLAIN RIGHT NOW.
Come along...
WE'RE HEADED UP TO THE NORTH COURT!!
And you'll find out right quick!
OH, HEYA, TAKAMI-SAN!
WHAT'S THE BIG FUSS ALL ABOUT? HAVE YOU FOUND THAT LITTLE GIRL, YET?
HUH ...?
THE NORTH COURT ?!
WHAT'S UP THERE ...?
Drat...
...I see...
THE NORTHERN SAKE COURT, HM?
THAT SOUNDS LIKE A PLACE FITTING FOR AN OKAMI-SAN TO VISIT.
LET US GO SEE, SHALL WE, SOU?
......
UH, SHE SAID "NORTH COURT," MIZUCHI-SAN. JUST "NORTH COURT."

Um...
BUT WHY?
WHY DO I HAFTA QUIT OUTTA TENCHI ACADEMY, HUH?!

IT'S ONLY NATURAL.
YOU GOT TOO CLOSE TO OUR AKIRA-SAMA.

AND THERE IS NO EVIDENCE TO SUGGEST THAT YOU WILL NOT ATTEMPT TO GET CLOSE TO HER AGAIN IN THE FUTURE.

In other words...
GETTING RID OF STUDENTS WHO BREAK THE TABOO...
IS THE JOB OF... THE A-TEAM!!!
FASH
Oooh...
I GET IT NOW ...!!!
Not.

NOW THAT WE ARE AT AN UNDER-STANDING, SIMPLY SIGN THIS WITHDRAWAL FROM COURSES FORM...
FWAP
EXCEL-LENT!!
AND THAT WILL SOLVE EVERYONE'S PROBLEM!!
OH, OKAY! WELL, IF THAT'S THE CASE--

I AIN'T SIGNIN' NOTHIN'!!!
WHOMP
OOPH!!
AAH! INDIRECT HIP!!
No way!
I'm so jealous!
KIKKAWA-SAMA! THAT WAS THE HIP THAT TOUCHED AKIRA-SAMA!!!
......
AH, WELL.
WE PLANNED FOR THE EVENTUALITY OF YOUR REFUSAL.
IT SEEMS...
YOU HAVE FORGOTTEN SOMETHING IMPORTANT, KUROGANE-SAN.
......!!
LIKE, PERHAPS, THE YOUNG GUEST WE CURRENTLY HAVE IN OUR CARE.
HERE, I HAVE A SWITCH.
NEED I TELL YOU WHAT THE BUTTON AT THE TOP WILL DO?
ONE PRESS AND THE DEVICE WE HAVE INSTALLED IN THE GUEST ROOM...
WILL ACTIVATE.
WHAT?!
WHAT'RE YOU GONNA DO TO MIKI?!!

SKFF
SKFF
IF YOU REFUSE, A MEMBER OF YOUR PRECIOUS FAMILY WILL GET A LITTLE HURT.
I TOLD YOU. THAT IS ENTIRELY DEPENDENT UPON YOUR ANSWER.
SKFF
ONLY WE KNOW WHERE SHE IS, SO THERE IS NO ONE TO RESCUE HER.
SKFF
IF YOU STILL REFUSE...
ALL OF THIS WILL BECOME OUR SHIELD AND YOU WILL BE THE ONE TO BE HURT.
YOU CAN'T TAKE ALL OF US DOWN. BUT DON'T WORRY, WE'LL SIMPLY KNOCK YOU OUT, PUT YOUR PRECIOUS SWORD IN YOUR HAND AND VOILA!
IF YOU SIMPLY SIGN THE FORM AND LEAVE THE ACADEMY, EVERYTHING WILL BE FINE.
HOW-EVER...
"SWORD BEARER LOSES CONTROL AND ATTACKS REGULAR STUDENTS!" IS THE NEWS HEADLINE OF THE DAY.
Most A-Team members are regular students, not sword bearers.
YOU BECOME THE CRIMINAL AND WE BECOME THE MVPs FOR TAKING YOU DOWN.
As for the girl, who cares?

NOT A BAD PLAN YOU'VE GOT THERE.
A-ha.
STOMP
AH...
EXCEPT FOR ONE THING.
YOU'RE EXPECTING KURO TO JUST ROLL OVER AND LET YOU BEAT THE CRAP OUT OF HER.
NOT HAPPENING. CLEVER TRICKS LIKE THAT DON'T WORK ON THAT MIDGET...
SHE'S TOO DUMB.
HAAAH HAAAH HAAH
AYANA-- !!!

CRAP!
HER SISTER-IN-ARMS SHOWED UP!
CALM DOWN. ONE OR TWO MORE PEOPLE AREN'T GOING TO AFFECT--
OI! YOU TWO!
YEAH, YOU TWO OVER THERE. YOU LOOK LIKE THE BRAINS OF THIS LOT.
WHAT SAY WE DO THIS NICE AND EASY.
YOU WANT KURO OUT OF THE ACADEMY, RIGHT?
WELL, OVER HERE WE'VE GOT TWO UNARMED SWORD BEARERS.
OVER THERE, YOU'VE GOT EIGHTY SWORD BEARERS AND REGULAR STUDENTS. GRAB WHATEVER WEAPONS YOU WANT...
AND BRING IT. ALL OF YOU.
IF ANY ONE OF YOU MANAGES TO LAND A HIT ON ME, WE'LL LEAVE THE ACADEMY OR WHATEVER ELSE YOU WANT US TO DO. HOW'S THAT SOUND?

HEH.
OH MY GAWD...
SNICKER
SHE'S A TOTAL IDIOT!
DOES SHE HONESTLY THINK SHE CAN WIN?! IT'S 80 ON 2!
WAIT--!!!
TA-DAH!
DON'T GO FOR-GETTIN' US!!
TEAMS KIBI-INUGAMI AN' KIJIMIYA-SAGARA ARE STEPPIN' IN ON KUROGANE'S SIDE!
ACROPHOBIC
H-hey! Quit it!
Stop pushing! I'll fall, you moron! I'll fall!!
GULP
YAMMER
......
LAST, AND PROB-ABLY LEAST, AN OKAMI AND A MAID.
Don't tell me you're still dragging that...!!
TCH ...!
Can we pull it off...?
NOW IT'S 80 VERSUS 8!
OH, SO NOW YOUR CONFI-DENCE STARTS FALLING APART...?

#32 END

Sou, from now on I shall call you SOU-SAN.

As is proper... for an okami to do.

DON'T! PLEASE!!

TENCHI ACADEMY

SWORD-BEARER LIST

■吉川 司(Kikkawa Tsukasa)■

High School, Class 1-B
Height: 161cm (5'3")
Weight: 50kg (110lbs.)
Birth Date: Mar. 30
Zodiac: Aries
Blood Type: A

High School, Class 1-B
Height: 160cm (5'3")
Weight: 51kg (112lbs.)
Birth Date: Sept. 11
Zodiac: Virgo
Blood Type: O

■布袋 朋(Hotei Tomo)■

●FILE EX.●

LEEEEEAN
PARDON ME...
HITSUGI-SAMA!
#33 Idiot Survival

......
PLEASE, LEND ME YOUR EAR. THERE IS SOMETHING I MUST TELL YOU.
NNNGH
......
TATEWAKI.
NNN
YOU ARE ENTIRELY TOO CLOSE.
Please, your ear. Need to hear...
Your ear, here... please...
HHNNN
SHEESH!
TAKE A STEP BACK.

BETTER.
YOU WERE SAYING?
YES, MISS.
BACK
I WAS MONITORING THE FESTIVAL ACTIVITY ACROSS THE CAMPUS VIA THE SECURITY CAMERAS...

WHEN I NOTICED A SUSPICIOUS GATHERING OF STUDENTS IN THE NORTHERN CLOCKTOWER COURT.
NO FESTIVAL ACTIVITY IS ANYWHERE NEAR THAT COURT.

KNOWING THE CURRENT SITUATION, AND THAT MEMBERS OF YOUR FAMILY ARE IN ATTENDANCE TODAY, I THOUGHT IT BEST TO INFORM YOU BEFORE THE NEWS REACHES THEM AND--

SHIZUKU.

YES, MISS?

LET US GO SEE TO THIS PERSONALLY.

I SEE.

UNDERSTOOD.

TAK

WE'RE MOVING OUT?!!

WAIT JUST ONE MOMENT, HITSUGI-SAMA!! I'LL BE READY TO GO IN AN INSTANT!!!

TOO CLOSE!

YOU STAY HERE, TATEWAKI.

WE CANNOT LEAVE THE STUDENT COUNCIL ROOM UNATTENDED, YOU KNOW.

ZWOOOM

#33 Idiot Survival

DUN
DUN
DUUUUN

YOU WIN. WE'LL GO WITH YOUR "SIMPLE" PLAN.

WE'LL DEAL WITH THE HOSTAGE LATER.

ALL RIGHT.

THERE ARE STILL 80 OF US, AND ONLY 8 OF YOU.

EVEN THOUGH THE MAJORITY OF OUR MEMBERS HAVE NEVER HELD A SWORD IN THEIR LIVES...

IT *IS* 80 VERSUS 8.

AS LONG AS YOU'RE SURE *YOU* ARE TRULY OKAY WITH IT.

WHAT SAY YOU STOP YOUR GABBING AND LET US GET THIS PARTY STARTED, HUH?

WHAT-EVER!

C'MON! I'LL THRASH EVERY LAST ONE OF YOU BEFORE YOU--!

CHAK

HOLD IT.

SO WHY DOES IT FEEL LIKE WE DON'T STAND CHANCE?!!

THAT'S RIGHT! WE HAVE 10 TIMES THEIR NUMBER!!

DA DA DA

GOOOONG

KIKKAWA, NO! DON'T BREAK BEFORE THE BATTLE'S EVEN BEGUN!!!

KIJI! WHAT GIVES?!
YOU BROUGHT YOURSELF HERE, GIRL. DON'T GO WUSSIN' OUT NOW!
THAT'S NOT IT.
YOU'RE JUST FORGETTING SOMETHING REALLY IMPORTANT.
Actually...
I ALMOST FORGOT IT MYSELF.
DRAW THAT AND IT'S A VIOLATION OF THE "NO SWORDPLAY OUTSIDE OF REGULATED TIMES" RULE.
No point to having it along at all.
THAT'LL MEAN DETENTION AND 12 OF YOUR STARS CONFISCATED.
AH ...!
Oh yeah...
EXACTLY.
DOESN'T MATTER WHAT WE DO, WE'RE ALL PRETTY MUCH UNARMED.
HEH.
NOT THAT WE'RE LIKELY TO NEED OUR SWORDS AGAINST THIS GAGGLE OF MORONS.
I MEAN, SERIOUSLY. THEY STARTED THIS THING WITH EIGHTY PEOPLE ALL TO TAKE OUT JUST ONE OF US.
DUST BUNNIES.
THAT'S WHAT THEY ARE: DUST BUNNIES AND HAIRBALLS. LIKE THE ONES YOU FIND UNDER YOUR BED.
I'LL... I'LL KIILLL YOU--!!!
Boof
WHOA!!
IT'S BEEN FOREVER SINCE WE LAST GOT TO HEAR ANY OF AYANA'S SCATHING INSULTS!

EVERY-ONE! READY YOUR WEAPONS !!
TO THOSE WITHOUT, THERE IS AN EQUIPMENT SHED WITH SPADES AND WRENCHES CLOSE BY!
WRENCHES?!
KIKKAWA... DON'T YOU THINK USING METAL WEAPONS IS GOING A LITTLE OVERBOARD ?!
JUST DO IT! WE NEED EVERY ADVANTAGE WE CAN GET!!
GLEAM
STOP RIGHT THERE.

WHA...
GLITTER
Where's that red light coming from...?
KA...
LADIES ...
KAICHO?!!!
GYAAAAA
THE FESTIVAL IS BACK THERE. WHAT ON EARTH ARE YOU DOING HERE?
HMM. I SEE MANY REGULAR STUDENTS AS WELL AS SOME OF MY SWORD BEARERS.
A candied apple...
That's a candied apple, right?
IF YOU HAVE GATHERED HERE IN THE HOPE OF... DEEPENING YOUR RELATIONSHIPS, SHALL WE SAY.
THEN I SHALL TAKE THE LIBERTY OF ASSUMING FORMAL COMMAND OF THIS...
SIDE EVENT.

FIRST, WE SHALL NEED SOME RULES.

AS THERE ARE A LARGE NUMBER OF REGULAR STUDENTS PRESENT, LET US MAKE THIS A MOCK HOSHITORI.

EACH STUDENT WILL NEED A STAR.

THESE STARS ALL HAVE THEIR HIT SENSORS TURNED OFF.

FUMP

For those students not in uniform...

Please use these.

IN OTHER WORDS, IT WILL NOT CALCULATE SPEED OR ACCURACY OF THE BLOW, YOU NEED SIMPLY TAP IT TO SET OFF THE BUZZER.

SWORD BEARERS, PLEASE SWITCH TO THESE STARS.

TMP

NEXT, WEAP-ONS--
ALL REGULAR STUDENTS AND RANK D SWORD BEARERS WILL RECEIVE PRACTICE BLADES.
KLOTTA KLOTTA
MURMUR
MURMUR
Er...
MY APOLO-GIES.
IN THE INTERESTS OF MAINTAINING FAIRNESS, THESE WERE THE ONLY APPROPRIATE WEAPONS I COULD FIND.
LADLES ...?
THOSE RANK C AND ABOVE...
WHO SEEM TO BE OVER THERE...
......
BWA HA HA HA HA HA!!!
NOW IT DOESN'T FEEL LIKE WE'RE A TOTAL LOST CAUSE!!
......
SO THOSE TWO ARE ONLY RANK D?
No wonder they looked... wimpy.
TA-DA

HN...
THINK ABOUT IT. COULD THERE BE MORE FITTING WEAPONS FOR US THAN THESE?
IN FACT, I BELIEVE I HAVE JUST LEVELED UP FROM A MERE OKAMI-SAN TO A MOTHER.
YES, THIS SEEMS VERY FAIR, DOESN'T IT, MUDOU-SAN?
Aaah...
Want miso soup with your spanking?!
AH...!
I get it.
How's it look?
A-AND A VERY LOVELY MOTHER YOU ARE, MIZUCHI-SAN!
TRUE.
SWISH
LADLES ARE PRETTY APPROPRIATE FOR A MAID.
HOW ABOUT FOR THE DUCK?
Think it'll work?
YUP!!
NO PROBLEMS HERE!!!

I MEAN, IF I LOSE, THEN I GET KICKED OUT AND I CAN'T PAY BACK DANDELION GARDEN'S LOAN!
BUT AYANA AND EVERYBODY'S HERE, SO THERE'S NOTHIN' FOR IT BUT TO WIN!!
RIGHT!
OH, BY THE WAY... IF WE DO MANAGE TO FIND SOME WAY TO LOSE, YOU'RE THE ONLY ONE WHO GETS EXPELLED, GOT IT?
Just thought...
I'd mention it.
SERIOUSLY ...?!!
ギョオ
GUAAAA
THE MATCH SHALL END ONCE ONE SIDE HAS SUCCESSFULLY STOLEN ALL OF THE OTHER SIDE'S STARS.
ANYONE WHO LEAVES THE CONFINES OF THIS COURT WILL BE DISQUALIFIED FOR GOING OUT-OF-BOUNDS. NO OBJECTIONS THEN?
WELL THEN...

BEGIN.
YAAAAAA
LET'S START WITH THE WEAKER-LOOKING ONES!
IF WE GO AFTER THEM ALL TOGETHER, THERE'S NOTHING TO BE AFRAID OF!!
YEAH! NOTHING TO BE AFRAID OF AT ALL!!
It's time for desperation tactics!!
SO LEAVE THE B RANKERS FOR LATER!
Especially the one in glasses!!
WHAT ?!
Isn't that back-wards?!
AGREED !! LEAVE THEM FOR LAST!!!

ANALYZ-ING...!!!
ジャキーン
SHIIING
TARGET... LOCK ON!!
!!
PURSUE ALL FIRST YEAR, RANK C GIRLS!!!

Here they come!
GO ON AND GO ALL OUT TODAY, WANKO!!
Here, hand me your ladle.
UM...
R-RIGHT...!!
Here.
MAX POWER...
BE THEE CURSED!!!
SHAZAM
SHAZAM
BREEEEEE
BREE
BREEEEEE

HN. NOT BAD, INUGAMI-SAN.
SWF
NOT MANY CAN CALL UP POWER WITHOUT A SWORD.
OF COURSE ...
I LIKE TO MANIPULATE THE ELEMENTS WITHOUT USING A PHYSICAL FOCUS, MYSELF.
The sword is just part of my training.
SWIFF
HERE... LET ME SHOW YOU THE *REAL* KIJIMIYA OTOHA.
SPIRITS OF LIGHTNING AND STORM, HEED MY--
WUH THE --?!!
Haaah!
Kyaaa!
BREEEEE
BREEEEE
BREEEEE
I SUMMON THEE.
MICHI ...
IS IT JUST ME, OR DID YOU SUDDENLY GET AWESOME?
y'know...
YEP!
FINALLY I'M USEFUL FOR A CHANGE! AND IT'S ALL THANKS TO THAT JEET KUN DO VIDEO COURSE.
I think I could get this to work with a sword...
SPARK
WAH-CHAA!
FOUNDER

OH MY GOD...
SKFF SKFF SKFF SKFF SKFF
Kyaaa!
Kikkawa-sama!
THEY...
Kyaaa!

THEY'RE ACTUALLY... GOOD!!!
HEY!! WHAT'S WITH THE DISBELIEF OVER THERE?!
GOOOONG

JUST BECAUSE WE'RE ONLY RANK C DOESN'T MEAN WE'RE WEAKLINGS WHO'LL LOSE THEIR STARS TO TOTAL *NOOBS!*

'SPECIALLY WITH KUROGANE'S FUTURE RIDIN' ON THIS!

Yes!

WHILE I DON'T HAVE ANY PARTICULAR OPINION ONE WAY OR THE OTHER ABOUT KUROGANE-SAN...

NO TRUE SWORD BEARER WORTH THEIR BLADE WOULD LOSE TO PEOPLE OF *YOUR* LEVEL.

HUH?

UH, KIJI-CHAN? YOU HAVEN'T STOLEN A SINGLE STAR YET.

BREEE
BREEE
BREEE
SO ANYWAYS...
WHAT'RE YOU ALL STILL DOIN' STANDING AROUND FOR?! BRING IT! I'LL TAKE ALL Y'ALL ON!!
WHOOOA ...
BOOOOOM
KYAAA !!!
HAAAAAAAAAAA
HN. LOOKS LIKE WE WON'T BE GETTING A TURN AFTER ALL.
AWE-SOME!
MOKA-CHAN AND EVERYONE'S GOTTEN REALLY STRONG!
THEY MUST'VE BEEN TRAINING WHILE WE WEREN'T LOOKING!
WHAT ABOUT ME, AYANA? WHAT ABOUT ME?!
DO YOU THINK I'M STRONGER NOW?!
WAAAAAAAA
......
WELL...
BOOOOM

WHAT SAY WE GO FIND OUT?
They aren't the best opponents, but ah well.
WHOEVER STEALS MORE STARS IS THE WINNER.
OOH!
YEAH! THAT SOUNDS LIKE A HOOT!!
IF YOU ARE IN THIS CON-TEST...
THEN I MOST DEFINITELY WISH TO PARTICIPATE AS WELL.
WHOA!
SHOULD I BE THE WINNER...
THEN I DEMAND YOU REMEMBER MY FULL NAME CORRECTLY!
GOT THAT, MUDOU-SAN?! YOU'D BETTER PROMISE!
Uh...
I-I'LL TRY...
Okay, everyone!
READYYYY ...!
GO !!!

WAAAAAA
No way... they're monsters!
We couldn't ever beat them!
Riiight.
All losers gather over here, please.
BREEEEE
BREEEEE
BREEEEE
HEH...
NO MATTER WHICH WAY YOU LOOK AT THIS, IT IS JUST A FRACAS.
HOPING IT COULD BE PASSED OFF AS AN OFFICIAL "SIDE EVENT" IS FUTILE.
KAICHO! WHY SAY THAT NOW?
Utterly useless.
WE HAVE ALREADY SET EVERY-THING UP SO THAT THIS IS--

AWW... DRAT!
LOOKS LIKE I MISSED OUT.
KUGA-SAN.
When did you arrive?
HI THERE, KAICHO-SAN.
GUESS I GOT HERE JUST A LITTLE TOO LATE, HUH?
IF YOU WOULD LIKE TO JOIN THEM, PLEASE FEEL FREE. IT WOULD BE PAR FOR THE COURSE.
My, my...
THAT SEEMS UNLIKE YOU.
You enjoy those sorts of things, do you not?
YOU DO KNOW THIS IS CURRENTLY BEING BROADCAST LIVE ON THE CAMPUS CCTV, YES?
Huh?!
IT IS?! FOR REAL?!!
YES.
NAH, I'LL PASS.
DON'T THINK THEY NEED MY HELP.
ALL RIIIGHT!! HERE COMES KUGA JUN-CHAAAAN!!!
ド!!
DOOOOOOM
GYAA!! MORE WEIRDOS!!!
AHA HA HA HA HA! ADD ONE NINJA AND YOU GET TWICE THE CHAOS!!
KAICHO! THIS ISN'T SUPPOSED TO BE FUNNY!!!
BREEE
BREEEE

......
AND WHAT'S THIS...?
THIS IS "SURVIVOR ~HOSHITORI~", A SPECIAL PRESENTATION BROUGHT TO YOU BY TENCHI ACADEMY VOLUNTEERS.
Sheesh, there sure are a lot of people wanting to jump in, today.
IT LOOKS LIKE A MYSTERY MAID-NINJA HAS JOINED THE FRAY!!
WAAAAAAAA!
WHICH SIDE WILL WIN? WATCH AND SEE!
WE HOPE YOU ENJOY THE SHOW.
DIRECTORY
Goldfish
Papa, is that who I think it is...?
....
OJOU-SAN...
YES?
BWA HA HA!! FEAR THE SLAYER OF ONE-THOUSAND ENEMIES!!
There're only eighty of them, you moron!!
MISS, IS THAT...?
YES. THAT'S JUN...
What does that doofus think she's doing?

WAS MY DAUGHTER ALWAYS THAT MUCH OF AN IDIOT?
UM ...
WELL...
Yeah, mostly...
YES!
WE HAVE LOTS OF VERY INTERESTING FRIENDS HERE!
OH. AH WELL...
AT LEAST SHE LOOKS LIKE SHE'S HAVING FUN.
AH! JUN'S ROOMMATE MUDOU-SAN JUST RAN ACROSS THE SCREEN.
OH, AND THE ONE IN THE DUCK-SUIT IS KURO-GANE-SAN.
?
TWITCH
THE ARROW GIRL...!
I CAN'T WAIT TO COME BACK HERE.
Mommy, Daddy, look! Oneechan!
BACK TO TENCHI.
......
I'M SURE IT WON'T BE ALL THAT LONG.
You'll be getting her cells, after all.

ME, TOO.
I HOPE YOU COME BACK REAL SOON, YUHO.
WITHOUT YOU AROUND, KUGA-SAN RANDOMLY DECIDES TO SLEEP IN MY ROOM SOME NIGHTS.
I DON'T MIND THAT PART ALL THAT MUCH, BUT THOSE... WEIRD VIDEOS SHE WATCHES...
That I mind.
SIZZLE
I'M SO SORRY, KEI-CHAN.
Lecherous little brat!
I'LL TRY TO GET BACK AS SOON AS I CAN. I PROMISE.
YUHO'S FORMER ROOMMATE KEI
ソーラン
*SOU-RAN
SWOOO
KRANG
WHOA ...!
BREEEEE
HNN ...
WHOP

......
THEY'VE ONLY GOT PRACTICE BLADES, BUT STILL. TAKING A DIRECT HIT WITH THIS DINKY THING IS A BAD IDEA.
It's only a skinny little ladle, after all.
THIS MIGHT BE A LITTLE MORE SEVERE A CHALLENGE THAN I THOUGHT.
AH WELL, I PROBABLY SHOULDN'T COMPLAIN. THIS'LL BE GOOD PRACTICE...
AYANA! HEY, AYANA!!
WHA ?!
THIS IS REALLY COOL!
IF I TRY TO BLOCK THEIR SWORD HEAD ON, MY LADLE WILL GET ALL BENT!
I'M SHORT 'N STUFF, TOO...
SO IT'S SOMETHING I PROBABLY NEED TO LEARN ANYWAY!
SO THIS IS A GREAT WAY TO PRACTICE REDIRECTING ATTACKS!!
SO THE LITTLE DIP DOES GET IT.
That's... discon-certing.

RIGHT!
SLIDING MY FINGERS UP, UP AND UP--!!!
LIKE SLIDING YOUR FINGERS UP AYANA'S THIGH!!
For example...
THAT'S IT, HAYATE-CHAN! EXACTLY!
YOU LET THEIR BLADE SLIIIDE ALONG YOURS, KILLING THEIR MOMENTUM AND POWER.
ぞわっ
SHUDDER
くけぇぇぇぇぇぇ
GURK!!
NGRAA-AAAAA-AAAA!!!
WOW! NOW THAT WAS A BEAUTIFUL DOUBLE LARIAT!!
WAIT...
THOSE THREE ARE ON THE SAME TEAM!
ONE OF THE MAIDS HAS TURNED ON HER TEAM-MATES!!
ぎゃあああぁ
GYAAAAAAA
....

......
WAAAA!
YES, SEMPAI?
ER... NOTHING.
I WAS JUST WONDERING IF YOU WERE MAD AGAIN...
You were scaring me for a second, there...
I'M NOT MAD. I'M EXASPERATED.
Always.
BUT I'M GETTING USED TO IT.
Boy, I'm tired.
AFTER ALL, THIS IS BETTER FOR HER THAN HOLING UP IN HER ROOM AND NEVER COMING OUT, DON'T YOU THINK?
I'M SURE SHE'LL BE BACK TO HER OLD SELF, SOON.
BUT FIRST, TOMORROW...
WE NEED TO TRY AND CHANGE OURSELVES.
......
I HOPE IT GOES WELL.

WHOA
WHOA
WAAAAAAA
WHOA
......

THIS IS BAD...

I KNEW THIS FROM THE BEGINNING, BUT...
HIYAAAA!
BOOOOOM
THOOOOOM
We're now down to under half our numbers.
WE ARE SERIOUSLY OUTCLASSED!!!

IN FACT, WE WERE DOOMED FROM THE INSTANT WE DECIDED TO PLAY FAIR!
DOOM

I GET HOW YOU FEEL, KIKKAWA, BUT WE JUST HAVE TO FORGET ABOUT THAT NOW! WE NEED TO GO FIGHT!!

RIGHT.
I FULLY INTEND TO FIGHT.

AS LONG AS WE HAVE THIS...
WE STILL HAVE A CHANCE TO WIN!
SO YOU'RE GOING TO USE IT AFTER ALL...

STOP RIGHT THERE, KUROGANE HAYATE!!
IF YOU AND YOUR FRIENDS DO NOT CEASE FIGHTING AND DROP YOUR WEAPONS IMMEDIATELY...
WOOSH
I *WILL* PRESS THIS BUTTON !!!
......!!
YOU DO REALIZE WHAT WILL HAPPEN, YES?
ALL I NEED DO IS PRESS THIS BUTTON...
...AND THE CASSETTE PLAYER WE HAVE HIDDEN IN THE STORAGE SHED WITH OUR HOSTAGE WILL TURN ON RECORDINGS OF *"INAGAWA JUNJI'S HORROR STORIES"* RADIO DRAMA SERIES AT FULL VOLUME!!
WHAT'S SO IMPORTANT ABOUT THAT BUTTON, KAICHO?
I HAVE NO CLUE.
In fact, what on earth started this whole mess in the first place?
SQUEEEEEE!!
キャアアアアアアア
WHA--?

HUNH.
SO THEY REALLY DO EXIST.
......
SO...
THE "FAN CLUB" THAT DEDICATED ITSELF TO THE GREAT MIKADO AKIRA-SAMA...
IS A BRAT PACK OF LOSERS WHO TAKE HOSTAGES AND THREATEN THEIR OPPONENTS?
DOOM
AKIRA-SAMAAAAA!!!
GOD, YOU SUCK. ALL OF YOU.
SWF SWF SWF SWF SWF
STMP STMP STMP STMP
I'VE SEEN ENOUGH. AS OF TODAY, YOU TRASH ARE DISBANDED. GOT IT?
BUT... BUT...
AKIRA-SAMA! THAT'S EXCESSIVE! WE WERE ONLY TRYING TO HELP YOU...!
QUIT FUTZING WITH YOUR GLASSES!!
SHF SHF SHF
SHUT IT!!!
GOOOONG

I'M NOT SO BAD OFF THAT I NEED YOU LOT TO DO ANYTHING FOR ME.
FWOOSH
What's goin' on?
Looks like an argument.
BUT IF YOU STILL WANNA KEEP THIS CRAP UP...
THEN YOU'RE GONNA BE FACIN'...

ME !!!!
AUGH!!!
CRAP, THAT'S RIGHT! TODAY I HAVE TO...!!
Silly Akira...
YOU COMPLETELY FORGOT WHY YOU WORE YOUR COAT, DIDN'T YOU?
AH.
IT'S ALL RIGHT...
WE HAVE NO REGRETS LEFT IN LIFE...
AT ALL.

HUH ...?
Oh my.
Genocide.
FWUUUUMP
WHAT THE-- ?!
HEY!! WHAT'RE YOU ALL JUST KEELING OVER FOR?!!
HOLEY MOLEY, LADIES AND GENTLE-MEN!!
THE NEWLY ARRIVED REBEL-MAID HAS JUST KNOCKED OUT ALL OF THE REMAINING GLASSES ARMY IN ONE BLOW!!
WHO COULD'VE SEEN SUCH A FINALE COMING ?!
KLANG KLANG KLANG
AHA HA HA HA HA HA!!
KLANG KLANG KLANG
MIKADO-SAN, THAT WAS PERFECT!!
K-kaicho...!
NOW ISN'T THE TIME FOR THAT!
HNH. LOOKS LIKE IT'S OVER.
Doesn't feel right...
Um...
SO WHAT HAPPENS TO ME NOW?
I'm not getting kicked out, right?
HOW ABOUT YOU GO GET THAT KID FIRST?
AL-READY RES-CUED.
UH, MINORI ?
Wait a sec...
WHO'S THIS KID BELONG TO?
I want pink and orange! Two-tone!!
I DUNNO. SHE WAS IN THE FOOD STORAGE ROOM.
KE-RUNCH KRUNCH KRNCH
SHE GAVE ME SOME CANDY, SO I BROUGHT HER ALONG.
ULTIMATE CRACKERS

#33 END

Do I really look that weird?

No, no. You look cute!

FWIF

Like someone's silly, pointless little hidden talent is cute.

GUIDE TO TENCHI ACADEMY

○ MIDDLE SCHOOL ○ RED WITH WHITE STRIPES

1ST YEAR 2ND YEAR 3RD YEAR

○ HIGH SCHOOL ○ WHITE WITH NAVY BLUE STRIPES

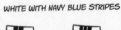

1ST YEAR 2ND YEAR 3RD YEAR

○ KUROGANE HAYATE ○

1ST YEAR 2ND YEAR 3RD YEAR

CLASS BADGES

#34 Idiot Interval

SEMPAI? SEMPA~I!
VICE CAPTAIN!
SHOOP
WHAT ALREADY, MIDDLE SCHOOLER?! DO YOU HAVE TO MAKE THAT MUCH NOISE THIS EARLY IN THE MORN?
We heard you the first time.
ACK!
I'm sorry.
Um...
I...
I WAS SETTING UP THE DISPLAY PIECES...

WHEN I NOTICED ONE REALLY BIG, NICE ONE LEFT IN THE STORAGE ROOM.
ARE WE REALLY NOT SUPPOSED TO PUT THAT ONE ON DISPLAY?
THAT'S THE CAPTAIN'S?
AH, THAT'S MAKI'S, RIGHT?
YEAH, THAT ONE DOESN'T GO ON DISPLAY.

SHE SAYS SHE DOESN'T WANT IT TO GO UP YET BECAUSE IT ISN'T COMPLETE.
WHA...?
NOT DONE...? *THAT...?!*
Yep.
SOMETHING ABOUT NOT BEING ABLE TO DECIDE ON THE RIGHT BLUE FOR THE SKY.
Whoa... no way...
SHE'S NOT ONE TO DO THINGS IN HALF-MEASURES, YOU KNOW.
THE NUMBER OF HER WORKS THAT MAKE IT INTO OFFICIAL EXHIBITS IS STAGGERING.
Wow.
THAT'S WHY SHE'S CAPTAIN A FULL TWO YEARS EARLY.

#34 Idiot Interval

Seriously.
SHE'S GOT INCRED-IBLE TALENT.
WHY SHE'D PUT THAT ALL IN DANGER WITH SOMETHING AS VICIOUS AS THE HOSHITORI, I HAVE NO IDEA...

TA-DA~!

CLAP

TENCHI ACADEMY SCHOOL FESTIVAL: DAY 2

HI THERE, LADIES AND, ER... *LADIES!*
WE'RE THE SWORD COMEDIENNE DUO "ONIGASHIMA!"
C'mon...
Introduce yourself.
......Hi......
I'M TAMA-KOCHI-GA-ONI.

AS YOU ALL SEE, WE'VE GOT THESE. THESE MAKE US SWORD BEARERS.
THAT'S WHY WE'RE IN THE SWORD COMEDIENNE CATEGORY, Y'KNOW!
THERE'S NO SUCH CATEGORY, YOU IDIOT!

SO I THOUGHT, HEY! WHY DON'T WE GIVE YOU ALL A *SWORDSMAN'S* COMEDY ROUTINE TODAY!
DITZ. HOW'S THAT COMEDY?
And who asked, huh?

TODAY'S SKIT IS ALL ABOUT *ASPARAGUS* WRAPPED IN *BACON.*
WHAT?!

I *LOVE* ASPARAGUS WRAPPED IN MEAT! BUT YOU SEE, I'VE GOT A PROBLEM... IT'S KINDA AWKWARD TO EAT.

SO I CAME UP WITH A GREAT *SWORDSMAN-ESQUE* IDEA!
Oh, great.
"SWORDS-MAN-ESQUE" ...?
EVERYBODY, LISTEN UP, OKAY? THIS IS A SUPER EASY, THREE-STEP WAY TO MAKE REALLY TASTY AND REALLY SIMPLE-TO-EAT ASPARAGUS AND BACON!
ZONY

OKAY, FIRST YOU WANT TO TAKE ASPARAGUS-SAN AND HIS LITTLE BUDDIES AND BOIL THEM A LITTLE. JUST A LITTLE, 'KAY?
THEN FOR STEP TWO, YOU TAKE THEM AND WRAP THEM IN THIN SLICES OF BACON AND FRY THEM UP.
Oh, don't forget to add salt and pepper to give it some taste.
THAT'S THE NORMAL WAY TO MAKE THEM.
NOW FOR THE GOOD PART! STEP THREE!
SLICE
YOU TAKE YOUR SWORD AND USE AN AIR-PRESSURE ATTACK TO SLICE ASPARAGUS-SAN INTO BITE-SIZED BITS WHILE STILL INSIDE THE MEAT!!
WHAT PART OF THAT IS SUPPOSED TO BE SUPER EASY?!!!
Looks just like any other asparagus and bacon...
but it's actually easy to eat!
WHAT, DO YOU THINK ALL JAPANESE HOUSE-WIVES ARE SECRETLY ELITE SWORD MASTERS?!
IF YOU WANT "EASY," JUST CUT THE DAMN THINGS BEFORE YOU WRAP THEM!!
Wait...
POW
KYAAAAAA!
......

UH, MOKA-CHAN?
WHAT PART OF THAT WAS THE PUNCH LINE?
I... KNOW THIS FEELING.
THE AIR IN THIS AUDITORIUM NOW IS ONE I KNOW WELL...
THE PART WHERE SHE BLEEDS ALL OVER EVERYTHING, OKAY.
IT IS CALLED "CRINGE-WORTHY," RIGHT, MOMOKA-SAN?
YEAH ...
That wasn't a funny joke, either!
All your jokes suck!
They're dumb, pointless and irritating!
SILENCE
GYAAA!
NICE VIOLENCE!
GYAAAAAA
....
UM...
SEMPAI ?

WHATEVER MADE YOU DECIDE TO COME WATCH THIS?
Classical music would have been more enjoyable...
I KNOW WE ARE REQUIRED TO ATTEND AT LEAST ONE VOLUNTEER PERFORMANCE, BUT THERE WERE MANY OTHER CHOICES...
YEAH, IT PROBABLY SHOULDN'T HAVE BEEN THIS ONE.
I'M SORRY. I DON'T HAVE MUCH OF A CLUE WHEN IT COMES TO THESE THINGS.
I THOUGHT MAYBE A COMEDY ACT WOULD BE THE THING TO HELP EASE MY NERVES...
But it's not. At all.
NERVES? YOU?
I DIDN'T THINK YOU EVER GOT NERVOUS, SEMPAI.
I'M SERIOUS, ACTUALLY.
IT ALWAYS SEEMED TO ME THAT YOU GO INTO OUR MATCHES CALM AND RESERVED.
THAT'S NOT ALWAYS THE CASE, YOU KNOW.
OF COURSE I DO! I'M HUMAN, JUST LIKE YOU!
ESPECIALLY THIS TIME, SINCE IT'S A "MUST WIN."
I'M NOT REALLY GOOD WITH THE TENSION THINGS LIKE THAT CREATE, TO BE HONEST.

MY MOTHER WAS THE ONE TO TEACH ME THE SWORD.
SO THAT'S ALWAYS THE WAY I'VE DONE THINGS.
Thank you! Thank you, everyone!
SO WHEN IT COMES DOWN TO IT, I'M NOT REALLY GOOD AT DO-OR-DIE SITUATIONS AT ALL.
CLAP
Pathetic, isn't it?
CLAP
CLAP
BUT SHE WAS NEVER ONE TO PRESSURE ME MUCH ABOUT WINNING MATCHES.
CLAP
...
Oh. Is it over?
SEMPAI ...?
YES?
Next, we have High School, first years--...
OWARAI ☆ GRAND PRIX
WHY DID YOU DECIDE TO PAIR WITH ME?
SHE SAID AS LONG AS I WAS HAVING FUN, THAT WAS GOOD ENOUGH.
YOU KNOW THAT ALREADY. I WAS BORED.
IF THAT WAS ALL IT WAS, YOU COULD HAVE PAIRED WITH ANY NUMBER OF OTHER PEOPLE.
WHY TAKE ME AND ALL MY BAGGAGE?

HMM...
WELL...
I'VE NEVER BEEN ABLE TO DECIDE ON THE RIGHT BLUE FOR THE SKY.
I GUESS...
BY PAIRING UP WITH YOU, YUKARI, IT FELT LIKE I WOULD FINALLY SEE THE RIGHT COLOR FOR IT.
UM...
DID YOU UNDER-STAND THAT?
......
UH, SORRY. NO. NOT AT ALL.
HEH. IT'S KINDA VAGUE, EVEN TO ME...

OH WELL.
THAT'S OKAY.
IT'S PROBABLY SOMETHING ONLY I WOULD UNDER-STAND.

WHAT I REALLY WANT TO KNOW...

YOU HAVE THINGS LIKE THAT TOO, RIGHT, YUKARI?

THINGS ONLY YOU CAN SEE, ONLY YOU CAN FEEL...

THINGS ONLY YOU COULD SHARE WITH SOMEONE ELSE.

IS HOW BLUE THE SKY WAS...

WHEN THE TWO OF YOU WERE TOGETHER.

I WAS THINKING THAT, IF I CAN GET PAST THESE NERVES...
THEN MAYBE I COULD FINALLY BE ABLE TO SEE THOSE THINGS THAT YOU DO.
THAT...
I DO...?
?
ER, WELL ...
UNFORTUNATELY, RIGHT NOW...
THANKS TO THAT COMEDY ACT A MINUTE AGO, ALL I CAN SEE IS MYSELF LYING IN A PUDDLE OF MY OWN BLOOD...
Hoo boy...
......
I TOLD YOU WE SHOULD HAVE CHOSEN SOMETHING ELSE!
BESIDES, JUDGES WILL BE WATCHING, SO WE'LL BE FINE.
I DON'T KNOW ...
WE'LL BE FINE!
...
ALL RIIIIGHT!!

ONCE LUNCH IS ALL DONE, IT'S BACK TO MASCOT LAND!
WE'LL SELL 300 CAT PASTRIES YET!!
I MEAN, WE'VE ALREADY SOLD 200 YESTERDAY!
MAKIN' 300 WILL BE CAKE!!
RIGHT.
YEAH!!
'COURSE, 40 OF THOSE 200 WE "SOLD" TO THE DANDELION GARDEN KIDS... *FOR FREE.*
BUT THAT'S NOT THE BEST PART!
ONCE THE FESTIVAL'S OVER, NEXT COMES THE **AFTER PARTY!!**
AND WITH THE AFTER PARTY, THERE'S GONNA BE A BIG BONFIRE, RIGHT?
AND THAT MEANS HOT, CLOSE FOLK-DANCING FOR ME AND AYANA!!!
KYA-HAAA!!
God, you're resilient...
NO WAY YOU DON'T GOT A REAL GOOD IDEA OF WHAT MUDOU-SAN'S LIKE, AND YOU CAN STILL MAKE UP FANTASIES LIKE THAT?
A BLAZING FIRE...
"OKLAHOMA WHATSIT" PLAYING SOFTLY IN THE BACK-GROUND...
PUFF
PUFF
Kuro...
Come on.
WITH ALL THAT ATMOSPHERE, EVEN AYANA'S GOT TO FEEL LIKE BEING A LITTLE NICER!
HEY, WHOA. WHOA! WHO'S *THAT* SUPPOSED TO BE?!
PUFF

FANTASY
WOW, AYANA. YOU, UM, SEEM A LITTLE DIFFERENT TODAY.
Hm?
REALLY?
WELL, TODAY IS SPECIAL, AFTER ALL.
HERE. GIVE ME YOUR HAND.
NOW HOLD ON, AND DON'T LET GO--
KRIK
POP
SNAP
KER RACK
REALITY
GYAAAAAAAAAAAAAA!!!
I SAID DON'T LET GO.
I'M NOT DONE CRUSHING ALL FIVE OF YOUR FINGERS INTO A USELESS, BLOODY PULP YET.

AYANA!!

INVADING MY INNERMOST DREAMS WITH SUCH VIOLENCE! I-I CAN'T SAY I'M SURPRISED, BUT...

Virtual pain!!

BUT STILL! *IT'S TOO MUCH!!*

THEN QUIT PROJECTING THOSE SHUDDER-INDUCING FANTASIES WHERE ANYBODY CAN SEE THEM, **DIMWIT.**

MEANIE!!

AND AFTER YOU WERE SO KIND DURING OUR DIRTY DANCING!!

AND QUIT MIXING UP THAT IMPOSSIBLE, DISGUSTING DREAM WITH REALITY!!!

BESIDES, THE AFTER PARTY DOESN'T HAVE ANY BONFIRES! AND NO DANCING, EITHER!

It's just a BBQ!

Aww~!

THAT'S NO FUN!

HN? WHAT'S WRONG, WANKO?

......

Disappointed

ANYWAYS, THAT ISN'T WHAT I CAME HERE TO TALK TO YOU ABOUT.
I WANT TO MAKE SURE OF SOME THINGS.
MAKE SURE OF WHAT?
THE HOSHITORI.
THERE'S A GOOD CHANCE THE BELL'S GOING TO RING TODAY.
BECAUSE TODAY'S A SCHOOL EVENT, IT'S NOT JUST ANY HOSHITORI, SO I'D USUALLY WANT TO PARTICIPATE, BUT NOT THIS TIME.

Hmm?
SURE, I'M OKAY WITH THAT. DIDN'T EXPECT TO HEAR YOU SAY IT, THOUGH.
DO YOU REALLY LIKE WEARING YOUR MAID DRESS THAT MUCH?
What, has your inner woman finally awakened?
SIGH
......
WHAT PART OF THAT PEA-BRAIN OF YOURS DID YOU USE TO COME UP WITH THAT REASON?

I'VE GOT TO MAKE UP FOR YESTERDAY.
A pain in the butt, but I do owe them...
THAT WHOLE HOSTAGE DEAL YESTERDAY KEPT ME BUSY THE WHOLE DAY. I WOUND UP NOT HELPING MY CLASS AT ALL.
AH!
OH YEAH... EVERYBODY WENT TO ALL THAT TROUBLE JUST TO HELP ME OUT YESTERDAY.
Aowwy...
HN? WOW. A PROPERLY REPENTANT ATTITUDE. RARE STUFF.
DON'T WORRY ABOUT IT, KUROGANE-SAN.
IT'S ONLY NATURAL FOR **FRIENDS** TO HELP **FRIENDS** IN TROUBLE.
TUNK
UGH. HER AGAIN...
......

SO, LOSER...
WHAT'S BROUGHT ON THIS 180-DEGREE FLIP-ABOUT IN OPINION FROM YESTERDAY, HM?
I do recall you saying somethin' like not havin' any particular attachment...
WELL, SINCE YOU ASKED...
HOW COULD I NOT, AFTER RECEIVING SUCH AN ADORABLE SYMBOL OF CAMARADERIE?
I *HAD* TO CHANGE MY MIND.
NYOOOHN
WHA——?!!

WAIT...
WH-WHAT'RE YOU DOIN' WITH ONE OF THOSE?!
KUROGANE!! WHAT THE HELL'S GOIN' ON HERE?!!
THEY'RE 'THANK YOUS' FOR YESTER-DAY.
I HAD SOME MADE UP ALREADY, SO I BROUGHT THEM THIS MORNING.
Thank you!
I GOT ONE, TOO! HER NAME IS SHIGERINE.
MIII
HM?
I'm workin' on one for Shisho, too.
HAD ONE MADE UP AL-READY?
AAH, I GET IT.
HEH
HERE, LET ME GIVE LITTLE MR. FACTORY-MADE THERE HIS NAME...
"LOSER."
IT'S KAZUSHIGE, FOR YOUR INFORMATION!! YOURS TOTALLY IGNORES THE NAMING CONVENTION!
WHAT, DON'T LIKE "LOSER"? HOW'S ABOUT "STALKER" THEN?
That's all it is.
SO THAT'S THE MASS PRO-DUCED VERSION.
IT ISN'T LIKE OURS.
HAH!
SHEESH. YOU'RE JUST A BALL OF SPITE AND VENOM TODAY, AREN'T YOU?
Here they go again...
MY, THOSE ARE SOME AWFULLY POINTED AND BARBED STATEMENTS YOU'RE MAKING...
I KNOW! IF YOU JUST ARRANGE IT A LITTLE, YOU GET "LOSER STALKER SHIGE-CHAN"!
LOSER☆STALKER SHIGE-CHAN
HOW'S THAT AR-RANGING ANY-THING?! YOU JUST SAID IT AS IT WAS!!
YOU were the one who named him that!!
AND WHAT HAPPENED TO "KA-ZUSHIGE"?

GOOD GRIEF ...
I CAN'T STAND THIS KIND OF CRAP. I'M OUTTA HERE.
ANY-WAYS, SEE YA.
Besides, who gave you the right to name my kitty mascot?!
GYAA
Well, I'm Kurogane's BEST FRIEND, so I get to do what I want, and I say he's "Loser"!!
GYAA
She was so happy to get it, she's been smiling all day!
My...
That's wonderful!
GYAA
OH YEAH...
DO YOU KNOW IF JUN-JUN'S GONNA BE STUCK IN CLASS ALL DAY, TOO?
If so, I'll set some pastries aside for her.
JUN?
Y'KNOW, I HAVEN'T SEEN HER ALL DAY, ACTUALLY.
I BET SHE'S JUST SLACKING OFF SOMEWHERE WHERE SHE CAN PEEP ALL DAY.
YEOW, WHAT A SHOCKER.
WAUGH!!
FSH
HOW LONG HAVE YOU BEEN STARING UP MY SKIRT?!
Yaay! Jun-Jun!
I WAS JUST CROUCHING, Y'KNOW. NO NEED TO BE SO MEAN.
SIGH
EVEN I HAVE TENDER FEELINGS THAT CAN GET HURT, AFTER ALL.
TO HAVE MISS "DOES-NOT-PLAY-WELL-WITH-OTHERS" HERSELF SAY THAT OF ME...
'SPECIALLY SINCE PAPA AND YUHO TOOK OFF YESTERDAY. BUT DID I HAVE TIME TO GRIEVE? NO. I'VE BEEN INFO-GATHERING ALL BY MY LONESOME ALL MORNING.
Papa...?
HUH?
TRANSLATION: YOU WERE OFF PEEPING ON SOMEONE EVEN AT THIS HOUR.
Do you get with-drawal symptoms if you don't peep?
UH, LET'S PUT THE WHOLE "PEEPING" SUBJECT OFF TO THE SIDE FOR A SEC, SHALL WE?

I WAS DOING SOME RECONNAIS-SANCE IN THE RANK SPECIAL A AREA.
RANK A AND UP EACH HAVE THEIR OWN SPECIAL, WALLED OFF SECTIONS, AFTER ALL.
Was tryin' to find an escape-route out...
SPECIAL A? WHAT FOR?
THAT RANK IS OUT OF YOUR RANGE, EVEN ON A DOUBLE UP DAY.
NO NO NO.
I'M NOT THE ONE PLANNING A CHALLENGE.
SOMEYA IS.
SHE AND KAMIJOU-SAN ARE THE ONES TAKING A SHOT.
PROVIDED THE BELL DOES RING.

BUT YUKARI JUST...
I MEAN THE TWO OF THEM JUST ADVANCED TO RANK A.
No...
YEAH. SHAKY BRIDGE OVER A DEEP CHASM, ISN'T IT?
BUT...
I HEAR THEY'VE GOT ONE SPECIAL SOMEONE THEY WANT TO TAKE ON.
....
JU ENSOO...
PROB-ABLY.
I CAN'T THINK OF ANYONE ELSE, ANYWAY.
Hm?
...
I'M GOING TO GO GET CHANGED.
Hmmm?
WHAT'S THIS?
NO REACTION? I'M NOT SAYING YOU NEED TO CHEER HER ON, OR STOP HER OR ANYTHING, BUT SOMEYA STILL DESERVES--
CAN'T.
NOT MY PLACE.
I DON'T HAVE THE RIGHT TO SAY ANYTHING TO HER RIGHT NOW.

WHOA ...
THAT WAS CHILLIER THAN EVEN I EXPECTED.
MAYBE I SHOULD'VE KEPT IT A SECRET AFTER ALL.
Kidding.
IS SOMETHING GOING ON WITH YUKARI-SAN?
HM?
OH. SHE'S PLANNING ON GETTING SOME REVENGE DURING THE NEXT HOSHITORI.
C'mon. Let's go outside for a sec.
THERE WAS THIS ONE PAIR THEY--BY WHICH I MEAN HER AND AYANA--LOST TO PRETTY BADLY BEFORE.
AH!
THAT WAS THAT ONE TIME, RIGHT?
WHEN THERE WAS THAT ACCIDENT WITH YUKARI-SAN'S FACE.
SOMEYA HERSELF IS SAYING SHE'S DOING IT TO COME TO TERMS WITH HER PAST.
AND IT LOOKS LIKE THAT'S THE WAY AYANA'S TAKING IT...
BUT ME, PERSONALLY? I THINK SOMEYA'S DOING IT ALL FOR AYANA.
URK.
UMM, WELL... THAT'S NOT EXACTLY IT, BUT YOU'RE CLOSE ENOUGH.
PLUNK
HUH?

LET'S PUT IT THIS WAY... AYANA SEEMED PRETTY UPSET ABOUT YUKARI'S SCAR, RIGHT?
YEAH. REALLY UPSET!
WELL, SHE USED TO BE A WHOLE LOT WORSE ABOUT IT BEFORE.
YOU'VE REALLY PUT YOUR MARK ON HER, HAYATE-CHAN.
THANKS TO YOU CHASIN' HER AROUND EVERY MINUTE OF EVERY DAY, SHE'S GOTTEN LOADS BETTER.
Even though you wind up getting beaten...
TURNS OUT THINGS WORKED A LOT BETTER FOR HER BECAUSE YOU DIDN'T KNOW ABOUT WHAT HAPPENED.
WHAT ?!
IF IT MEANS AYANA'S GONNA FEEL BETTER, THEN I'LL SPEND THE REST OF MY WHOLE LIFE NOT KNOWING A SINGLE THING!!!
IGNORANCE IS MY SPECIALTY!!
UM...
Y'KNOW? I THINK IT MIGHT BE A GOOD IDEA IF YOU STARTED TO LEARN A LITTLE BIT ABOUT IT...
FOR ONE...
JUST LIKE YOU ARE...
SOMEYA'S WORRIED ABOUT AYANA.

SHE WANTS AYANA TO STOP FEELING SO BAD ABOUT WHAT HAPPENED.
SO IN ORDER TO SHOW AYANA THAT SHE'S TOTALLY OVER IT...
SHE *PURPOSELY* PICKED OUT THE PAIR THAT BEAT THEM BEFORE...
SO THAT SHE CAN FIGHT THEM AND *THIS* TIME WIN.
WELL...
THAT'S WHAT I'M THINKING ANYWAY. DON'T QUOTE ME ON IT.
THEN...
THAT MEANS YUKARI-SAN *DOESN'T* HATE AYANA?
Nope!
SHE DOESN'T HATE HER AT ALL. THAT I KNOW FOR SURE.
SO THEN, WHEN YUKARI-SAN SEES AYANA AND MAKES ALL SORTS OF SNARKY INSULTS UNTIL AYANA'S ALL PALE AND SHAKY, IT'S *NOT* BECAUSE SHE HATES HER?
UMMMM...
YEAH, I'M PRETTY SURE I CAN SAY THAT'S NOT BECAUSE SOMEYA HATES HER...
IT'S A FETISH, MAYBE...

AND EVERY TIME SHE LOOKS AT ME WITH COLD DEAD EYES, IT'S NOT BECAUSE SHE HATES ME, RIGHT?!!
UHHH~...
DUNNO ABOUT THAT ONE. SHE KINDA LOOKS AT ME IN THE SAME WAY...
OH WELL!
IT DOESN'T REALLY MATTER WHAT SHE THINKS ABOUT ME ANYWAYS.
BOING
WOOHOO!! I'M SO HAPPY!!!
I'M GONNA GO GET CHANGED, TOO!
THANKS FOR TELLING ME THAT, JUN-JUN!!
DASH
BWAH ?!
That's it?
O-OH...
UH, OKAY.

SHE'S GOT A POINT.

IT IS SOMETHING WORTH BEING REAL HAPPY ABOUT.

I'VE GOT A REQUEST FOR YOU.

IF I REMEMBER CORRECTLY, ONE OF YOU CAN--

......

MAKI...
I'M REALLY SORRY.
I LIKE THE SWORD. I REALLY DO.
BUT THERE'S SOMETHING ELSE I LIKE MORE.
THE ACADEMY HAS PLENTY OF COURSES FOR ME TO STUDY IT...
BUT I'M AFRAID I WON'T BE ABLE TO CHOOSE BETWEEN THAT AND THE SWORD. SO I'M GOING TO LEAVE.

I WISH I WAS LIKE YOU, AND COULD BALANCE THE TWO SO EASILY.
BUT I'M NOT. I'M SORRY.

I'M NOT BALANCING THEM, REALLY.
I JUST CAN'T SEEM TO CHOOSE BETWEEN THE TWO.
IF I TAKE UP THE SWORD, I WORRY ABOUT MY DRAWING HAND.
BUT IF I TAKE UP THE PEN, I FIND MYSELF THINKING ONLY OF THE SWORD.
At this rate, this piece will never be done.

I WISH I COULD BE MORE LIKE THOSE TWO.
TO BE SO SURE, SO CERTAIN...

OF THE ONE THING THEY TRULY WANT TO MASTER.

!......
UM...
YOU ARE KUROGANE-SAN, CORRECT? SO, ER...
WHAT ARE THESE?
CAT PASTRIES, MA'AM!
TOASTY
HOT
I... CAN SEE THAT.
BUT... WHY GIVE THEM TO ME?
QUA!
SO YOU DON'T GO HUNGRY!
THEY SAY EMPTY STOMACHS ARE LIKE IKUSHIMA HIROSHI, AFTER ALL!
SO, NO NEED TO STAND ON FORMALITY FOR MY SAKE, MA'AM! TAKE THEM! PLEASE!!
......
AND AYANA IS TALKING TO THIS EVERY DAY?!
QUACK!!
SLUMP

Uhh...
ANY-WAY...
Um...
I-IF YOU DON'T REALLY HATE AYANA 'N ALL...
I guess... maybe...
soulmates is it...?
HUH?
AS A FRIEND OF A FRIEND, I CAN SUPPORT YOU ON THIS ONE.
Oh.
OH, JUN...
I'M SORRY, BUT YOU HAVE THE WRONG IDEA. I'M NOT--
AS AYANA'S CURRENT SISTER-IN-ARMS...
IT DOESN'T MATTER !!
AND SINCE YOU REALLY DO LIKE AYANA LOTS, I'M TOTALLY, 100% BEHIND YOU FOR HER!!
......
WHA-- ?!

SNAP
YEOWCH!
WHONK
SWOOM
ANY-WAYS!
I'VE GOTTA GO, SO GOOD LUCK!!
murmur
murmur
WHAT'D YOU DO THAT FOR?!!
THAT'S MY LINE!!!
YOU'RE NOT SUPPOSED TO THROW FOOD!
OH, DON'T WORRY! I'LL EAT IT!
I'LL EAT EVERY SINGLE LAST PASTRY IN THIS BAG!
Really?
Whatever! Just take back what you said a moment ago before you leave!
Wow, Yukari. You're an awfully thoughtful person!
And it's "Yukari-SAN"! Don't just call me by my first name. It's rude!!

WOING
WOING
WAP
EN-SOO.
IS THAT TRULY THAT ENTERTAINING FOR YOU?
SINCE WE ARE SKIPPING CLASS ANYWAY, WHY NOT GO ENJOY THE FESTIVAL SOME MORE?
WOING
Perhaps some place other than the yo-yo booth.
WAP
WAP
Vicious Animal Attacks
......
WHAT?
YOU WANT TO FIGHT THEM NOW?
MY, SUCH PETULANCE. YOU ARE NOT USUALLY LIKE THIS.
......
瞑子 メイ
<MEI.>
....
DON'T WORRY. THEY WILL BE HERE SOON.
I think.
THEN YOU CAN PLAY AS MUCH AS YOU LIKE.

#34 END

◦CAT PASTRY DIAGRAM◦

TENCHI ACADEMY

SWORD-BEARER LIST

■ DATA ■

High School, Class 2-E

Height: 163cm (5'4")

Weight: 51kg (112lbs.)

Birth Date: Aug. 17

Zodiac: Leo

Blood Type: O

Favorite Food:
meat, fish

■朱 炎雪(Ju EnSoo)■

●FILE21●

#35 Idiot Rival

I guess it's okay to eat.
The one I threw.
......
IT'S OBVIOUS THAT JUN HAD A HAND IN THIS.
SHE MUST HAVE CONVINCED HER THAT I'M DOING THIS FOR AYANA'S SAKE.
I CAN'T TELL IF I SHOULD CONSIDER HER HONEST, BLUNT...
OR JUST TRULY AND COMPLETELY STUPID.
YO!
She was dressed funnily, too..!
TO THINK OF BRINGING THESE...
EVEN FOR ME.
IT'S NOT WHAT SHE THINKS...

#35 Idiot Rival

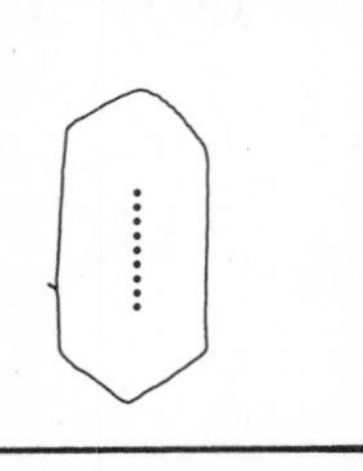
....

I CAN'T SAY I DIDN'T SEE IT COMING.
I JUST DIDN'T EXPECT IT SO SOON.

FROM THE DAY THAT HAPPENED...
SHE MUST NEVER HAVE STOPPED THINKING ABOUT IT.

SHE NEVER STOPPED WANTING...
TO FIGHT HER AGAIN.

THE WHOLE POINT OF ME SPLITTING UP WITH HER WAS TO KEEP THIS FROM HAPPENING.

I DON'T WANT HER TO EVER HAVE TO GO THROUGH SOMETHING LIKE THAT EVER AGAIN.

I CAN'T BELIEVE MAKI-SAN'S WILLING TO HELP HER OUT.

NEITHER OF THEM HAVE THE FIRST CLUE.

SHE...

——你呢
<YOU.>
是这里的人吧？
<YOU ARE ONE OF US, AREN'T YOU?>
SOMEWHERE, DEEP INSIDE OF US, SOMETHING BLACK AND UGLY HIDES.
SHE'S LIKE ME.

JUST...
LIKE...
AYA-
NA!!!
KLANG
KLATTER
WOOGA
WOOGA...
......

Ayana!
MUDOU-SAN?
WOOGA
ARE YOU OKAY? ARE YOU FEELING SICK?

I'M FINE. I GOT A LITTLE DIZZY, THAT'S ALL.
IT'S NOTHING.
OH.

SO STAY AWAY.

AH

TH-THAT'S GOOD. STILL, I THINK IT MIGHT BE A GOOD IDEA IF YOU TOOK A BREAK.
MAYBE GO OUTSIDE, GET SOME FRESH AIR. YOUR BLACK AURA IS SCARING THE CUSTOMERS.
SORRY ...
I think we came by at the wrong time again, Kei-chan...
Yeah...

IF YOU GET TOO CLOSE... THEN...

FIGH

MER-MAID Cafe

3-G

Maid Café

SOMETHING IS GOING TO BREAK.
BUT... EVERYTHING WILL BE FINE IF THE BELL DOESN'T RING.
IN FACT...
IT PROBABLY WON'T RING TODAY. THAT'S RIGHT.
CHANCES ARE TOO LOW.
NO WAY IT'S GOING...
TO...

GOOOOOOONG
....
What, the Hoshitori?
No way!
PASTRIES

......
——等你半天了
<I WAITED. NOW YOU COME.>
是同胞啊……！
<YOU WHO ARE LIKE ME.>
OOONNG
SEMPAI!
I'M SORRY I TOOK SO LONG.
IT'S ALL RIGHT. LET'S GO.

THOUGH, IT IS A GOOD WAYS FROM HERE TO THE RANK A AREA.
IT LOOKS LIKE OUR MATCH WON'T START UNTIL THE NEXT BELL.
AH WELL.
AGAINST OPPONENTS OF THEIR CALIBER, THE FIGHT IS GOING TO BE SHORT SO IT DOESN'T MATTER.
YES, IT WILL BE A SHORT ONE...
WIN OR *LOSE.*
"OR LOSE"?
I THOUGHT WE WERE GOING TO WIN THIS ONE NO MATTER WHAT.
YOU KNOW, SEMPAI? YOU MAKE IT REALLY DIFFICULT TO TELL HOW CONFIDENT YOU ARE IN SOMETHING.
OH, I SIMPLY PREFER TO TAKE THE POSITION THAT'S AT ODDS WITH YOURS. THAT'S ALL.
...
MY...
YOU LOOK TERRIBLY EXCITED TODAY.

INORI-SAN...
WHAT ARE YOU DOING ALL THE WAY OUT HERE?
This is the middle of the Rank A area.
JUST DOING MY PATROLS. THEY ARE PART OF MY RESPONSIBILITIES AS A STUDENT COUNCIL MEMBER, AFTER ALL.
THOUGH, I'M AFRAID I HAVE TO ASK YOU WHAT *YOU'RE* DOING HERE.
YOU WEREN'T SKIPPING, WERE YOU?
You got here entirely too quickly...
To be coming from any class area.
HONESTLY? YES.
DON'T BE TOO HARD ON US, WILL YOU? THE BELL HAS ALREADY RUNG AND ALL.
WAP
BESIDES, ONCE MY PARTNER GETS AN IDEA IN HER HEAD, SHE DOESN'T LET IT GO.
I see...
YOU REALLY ARE PLEASED BY HER, AREN'T YOU, HIMURO-SAN?
YOUR *CURRENT* ONE, THAT IS.
YES.
THOUGH, I DON'T KNOW WHAT YOU ARE IMPLYING.
AH, YES!
ABOUT THE AKIRA FAN CLUB...
IT WAS DISBANDED.
OH...
MY, MY... WHAT A BLAND REACTION.

HOW ELSE WOULD I REACT? I HAD NEITHER CONNECTION TO NOR INTEREST IN IT.
THAT IS A MISCONCEPTION KIKKAWA LIKES TO CLING TO, I'M AFRAID.
SHE MAY BE RELATED TO ME, BUT SHE DOESN'T SEEM TO HAVE INHERITED ANY OF THE FAMILY'S INTELLIGENCE, YOU SEE.
REALLY? NOW THAT'S ODD.
AND HERE I HEARD YOU WERE THE CLUB'S FOUNDING MEMBER.
The legendary Member OO.
ALL SOMEONE NEED DO IS PLANT A LITTLE IDEA IN HER HEAD, AND SHE WILL DO ANYTHING.
She especially listens to me.
WAP
WAP
WAP
IT SEEMED TO ME THAT SHE QUITE ADORED MIKADO-SAN...
SO I PRETENDED TO BE SIMILARLY INTERESTED AND PROMPTED HER INTO THE IDEA.
THE MOST AMUSING PART WAS THE GLASSES.
ALL I SAID WAS, "NOW I CAN SEE MIKADO-SAN CLEARLY, EVEN FROM FAR AWAY." SHE LATCHED ON TO THE SUGGESTION IMMEDIATELY.
WITHIN A FEW DAYS, IT WAS MANDATORY FOR ALL THE CURRENT MEMBERS TO WEAR THEM.
THE SILLY GIRL NEVER EVEN REALIZED THAT MINE WERE FAKE. IT WAS HILARIOUS.
I UNDERSTAND COMPLETELY.
YOU ARE THE KIND OF PERSON WHO ENJOYS MESSING AROUND WITH OTHER PEOPLE'S FEELINGS FOR YOUR OWN ENTERTAINMENT, AREN'T YOU, HIMURO-SAN?
Ha ha!
PLEASE, CALL IT "OBSERVATION."

I FIND AN AMUSING SUBJECT, INDUCE IN HER A COURSE OF ACTION, AND THEN OBSERVE THE RESULTS.
IT'S A STUDY OF HUMAN BEHAVIOR.
WAP
メイ
<MEI.>
AH. IT SEEMS OUR OPPONENT FOR TODAY HAS ARRIVED.
I'M SORRY, BUT OUR CONVERSATION IS AT AN END.
YES, I MUST BE ON MY WAY AS WELL.
BUT I THANK YOU FOR THE CHANCE TO CONFIRM THINGS.
I AM NOW VERY GLAD THAT I WAS THE ONE TO MEET AKIRA FIRST AND NOT YOU.

HM?
YOU LIED WHEN YOU SAID YOU WEREN'T INTERESTED, RIGHT?
I DON'T THINK I COULD STAND THE THOUGHT OF AKIRA BECOMING YOUR *TOY*, AS WELL.
YOU DON'T SEE OTHER PEOPLE AS HUMAN BEINGS, JUST AS PLAY-THINGS.
YOU'RE A PERFECT MATCH, YOU AND YOUR SISTER-IN-ARMS.
IN SOME WAYS, I'M A LITTLE JEALOUS.
BUT, YOU KNOW, WHEN ALL IS SAID AND DONE...
I CAN'T REALLY FIND IT IN ME TO SUPPORT YOU.
......
THAT'S PRECISELY AS I PREFER.
DMP
DMP
DMP

GOOOOOOONG
SEM-PAI...!
LOOKS LIKE WE MADE IT JUST IN TIME FOR THE SECOND BELL.
LET'S DO THIS IN ONE SHOT, YUKARI!
DON'T LET ANY OPPORTU-NITY GET AWA--
...!

WOOSH
SEM--!

!!
WAP
POP
PLSH
WHA ?!
WHR!
KRAK

GRSH
YUKARI!!
SWISH

WSH
UNGH!
WHD!!
SHF
RGK ...!
OH DEAR ...
I SEEMS THAT ONE WAS A LITTLE TOO FAR TO THE SIDE.
SKSHHH

KLATTER
DOOOOOM
...
SOMEYA-SAN. IT HAS BEEN TOO LONG.
THANK YOU SO MUCH FOR JOINING US, TODAY.
WE HAVE BEEN WITHOUT A CHALLENGE FOR SO LONG THAT MY PARTNER WAS GETTING TERRIBLY *IRRITATED*.
I APPRECIATE THIS.
I WOULDN'T TREAT THIS AS A GAME, IF I WERE YOU.
YOU MIGHT GET *HURT*.
MY, TO HEAR THOSE WORDS COMING FROM *YOU*.
A GRAVE WARNING, INDEED, CONSIDERING YOUR PAST.

......
HM?
AH...
MY PARTNER HAS A QUESTION FOR YOU.
SHE WOULD LIKE TO KNOW WHY YOU DO NOT HAVE THE SAME SISTER-IN-ARMS AS BEFORE.
!
JUST A LITTLE CHANGE OF PACE, THAT'S ALL.
WHAT, AM I NOT GOOD ENOUGH FOR HER?
No, no.
IT'S OKAY. DO NOT WORRY ABOUT IT.
SWIP
SHE ISN'T A PARTICU-LARLY *FUSSY* CHILD.

Hup
Hup
PROVIDED, OF COURSE, THAT YOU ARE...
"FUN TO PLAY WITH."
DMP
Hup
Hup
Hup
......
Hup
PUT ME DOWN !!!
Hup

HEY!
WHAT THE HELL DO YOU THINK YOU'RE DOING, ANYWAYS?!
HUP
HUP
STOP!! I'M IN NO MOOD TO PLAY WITH YOU TWO BEAN-BRAINS RIGHT NOW!!!
And put me down!!
HUP
TAKOYAKI
OKONOMIYAKI
REAL SORRY, MUDOU-SAN, BUT NO CAN DO. WE'RE IN A BIT OF A HURRY, Y'SEE.
HUP
ATTACK SQUAD
I GET THAT PART! TELL ME WHERE WE'RE GOING FIRST!!!
This is kidnapping, you know!!
WE'RE GOING TO GO SEE YUKARI, AYANA!
THAT'S "YUKARI-SAN" TO YOU, YOU RUN--
WAIT, WHAT?!!
Umm...
SORRY... ORDERS ARE JUST TO BRING YOU, NOT SAY ANYTHING ABOUT WHERE WE'RE GOING.
WHAT DO I NEED TO GO THERE FOR?!
WE AREN'T EVEN ALLOWED INTO THE RANK A AREA!!
HUP
HUP
WELL, WE'VE GOT A CONTINGENCY PLAN FOR THAT, ACTUALLY...
FWISH
HM?
FOG...?
BUT I DIDN'T SENSE ANYONE HERE JUST A MOMENT AGO.

DO YOU THINK THIS'LL DO?

What with Inugami-san amplifying it for me, and all...

FWIIIISH

I'M PRETTY CERTAIN WE HAVE ENOUGH TO BLIND ALL THE CAMERAS THROUGH THE WHOLE AREA.

Yes.

INFILTRATION SQUAD

YOU KNOW, THIS DOES PUT US IN THE MOST PRECARIOUS SPOT OUT OF EVERYONE.

And we're blowing off our class responsibilities again, too...

IF A JUDGE CATCHES US, WE'RE TOAST.

IT WILL BE ALL RIGHT, KIJIMIYA-SAN.

I WILL HANDLE ANY JUDGES.

FASH

ANY UNFORTUNATE ENOUGH TO WANDER TOO CLOSE SHALL BE **CURSED** BEFORE THEY SPY US!!

......

THAT'S REASSURING AND *FRIGHTENING* ALL AT THE SAME TIME.

OOOOH!

YOU TWO REALLY ARE TOTALLY COOL!

REALLY?

Y-YOU THINK SO?

Yes, it was!

I COULD NEVER, *EVER* DO SOMETHING LIKE THAT, SO IT LOOKS REALLY COOL TO ME!

GOOD LUCK, KIJI-CHAN! WAN-WAN! YOU CAN DO IT!

Erm...

THAT REALLY WASN'T THAT BIG A THING AT ALL...

CLAP CLAP

CHEERLEADING SQUAD

SO, UH, AS YOU CAN SEE, WE HAVE THAT SIDE OF THINGS PRETTY MUCH HANDLED.
YOU LUNATICS GET CAUGHT AND THERE'S NO TELLING WHAT THE KAICHO WILL DECIDE TO DO TO YOU.
DON'T GOT MUCH OF A CHOICE, REALLY.
AN' AFTER HEARING THE TRUTH ABOUT WHAT'S GOIN' ON FROM KUGA-SAN... WELL...
YOU CAN'T EXPECT ME TO KICK BACK AND WATCH, NOT AFTER THAT.
HUP
HUP
HUP
THE "TRUTH"?
I MEAN, WE'RE TALKIN' ABOUT YOU, HERE. YOU'RE KUROGANE'S SISTER-IN-ARMS.
I MEAN... YOU FINALLY MET HER!
AFTER BEING SEPARATED YOUR WHOLE LIVES!
......
Uh, excuse me...
WHAT THE HELL DID JUN TELL YOU?
AND THE 2,000 YEARS OF YOUR PREVIOUS LIVES, TOO!!
Is that supposed to be about me?
DON'T GIVE UP, MUDOU-SAN! LIVE!! YOU CAN MAKE IT!!
BAWL
SO JUN'S THE ONE BEHIND THIS WHOLE FARCE, HUH?
ALL RIGHT, PUT ME DOWN. I'VE GOT TO GO BEAT THE TAR OUT OF A CERTAIN MED-DLING NINJA...
HANG ON, AYANA!

JUN-JUN'S TAKING OVER FOR YOU AT YOUR, CLASS CAFÉ BOOTH-THINGY RIGHT NOW.
SHE JUST REALLY WANTS TO LET YOU WATCH YUKARI'S HOSHITORI BATTLE THIS ONE TIME.
Heya! I'm here to mate with... I mean, switch places with Ayana.
A-ha! There you are!
Kuga-chi! Stop being such a slacker!
AND I THINK IT'S A GOOD IDEA, TOO.
IF YOU REALLY, REALLY DON'T WANNA, THEN YOU CAN BEAT US UP FOR IT LATER.
BUT LET'S GO CHEER HER ON, FIRST!
IT'S NOT THAT I DON'T WANT TO. IT'S...
WHAT-EVER.
TAKE ME THERE IF YOU WANT, I DON'T CARE.
HEAR THAT, MOKA-CHAN? LET'S PUT THE PEDAL TO THE METAL!
YEAH!!
RIGHT YOU ARE! LET'S GO GO GO!!
OF COURSE, THIS DOESN'T MEAN I'M NOT GOING TO BEAT YOU BOTH FOR IT.
You're all gonna get the ass-bat at fullswing.
GAK?!!

KRAK
WHAT'S WRONG, SOMEYA-SAN?
SKSHHH
IT SEEMS THE ONLY THING THAT HAS IM-PROVED MUCH SINCE OUR LAST MATCH IS YOUR MOUTH.
WSH
STILL HAVING PROBLEMS ADJUSTING YOUR *VISION*, PERHAPS?
IS IT TOO HARD TO FOLLOW A BETTER OPPO-NENT'S MOVES?
IT'S NOT THAT I CAN'T FOLLOW YOU.
GOOOOOOOOONG
TAKE THIS THEN --!!
NGH !!
KRAK
WELL THEN, YOU HAD BETTER STOP ME SOON...

OR YOUR NEW SISTER-IN-ARMS OVER THERE JUST MAY WIND UP...
WITH HER PRECIOUS RIGHT HAND *BROKEN.*
WHA--?!
WORRIED?
MY PARTNER HAS KNOWN SINCE THE VERY BEGINNING.
I SIMPLY DIDN'T INTERPRET IT FOR YOU WHEN SHE MENTIONED IT BEFORE...
BUT SHE MOST DEFINITELY SAID THAT SHE WANTS TO *CRUSH* HER, STARTING WITH THE HAND SHE FAVORS SO MUCH.
SEMPAI--!!
WOOSH

SKSHHHH
NH ....!
SLINGING IT AT ME AGAIN?
WELL, SORRY, BUT THAT MOVE ISN'T GOING TO WORK ON ME MORE THAN ONC--
FWIP
......!!!
WHIRL
#35 END

HAYATE
HAYATE CROSS BLADE
BLADE

TENCHI ACADEMY

SWORD-BEARER LIST

■ DATA ■

High School, Class 2-E
Height: 168cm (5'6")
Weight: 54kg (119lbs.)
Birth Date: Oct. 19
Zodiac: Libra
Blood Type: A
Favorite Word: fabrication

■氷室瞑子 (Himuro Meiko)■

●FILE22●

#36 Idiots Struggle

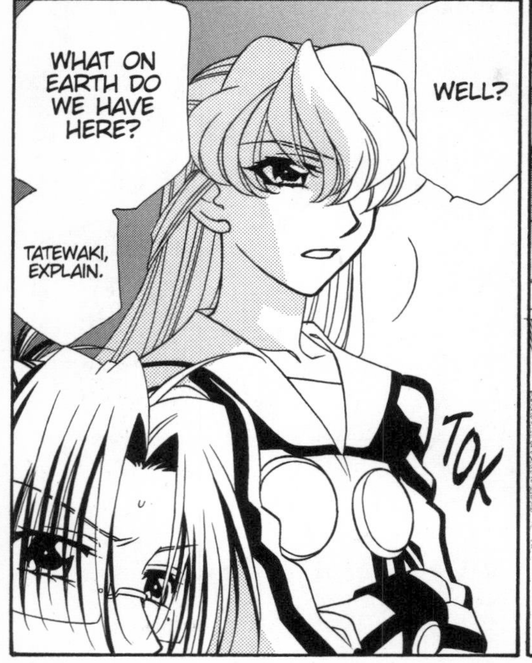

WHAT ON EARTH DO WE HAVE HERE?
WELL?
TATEWAKI, EXPLAIN.
TOK

TAK
TAK

I... I AM NOT CERTAIN, MISS.
IT APPEARS THAT SOME KIND OF THICK FOG HAS ROLLED IN, OBSCURING THE VIEW OF OUR SECURITY CAMERAS.
HOWEVER, STRANGELY, THE PHE-NOMENON SEEMS CONFINED TO THE RANK A AREA ONLY.
AMACHI

SO IT IS SAFE TO SAY...

THAT THIS IS SOME SORT OF DELIBERATE SABOTAGE ATTEMPT, CORRECT?

MAYBE...

SHALL WE HALT THE HOSHITORI?

EVEN OUR GPS IS NOT FUNCTIONING PROPERLY. JUDGES WILL NOT BE ABLE TO LOCATE AND PRESIDE OVER MATCHES.

THAT COULD BE DANGEROUS.

......

Hmm...

HITSUGI-SAMA...?

#36 Idiots Struggle

BE THAT AS IT MAY, RIGHT NOW IT IS BEST THAT WE SIMPLY KEEP AN EYE ON THE SITUATION.
INORI-SAN IS CURRENTLY PATROLLING THE RANK A AREA. SHOULD AN INCIDENT ARISE...
SHE SHOULD BE ABLE TO RESPOND.
BE-SIDES, ONLY TWO BELLS REMAIN.
WITH ONLY THAT MUCH TIME LEFT, THIS SITUA-TION IS BEST LEFT IN THE HANDS OF THE JUDGES AND SWORD-BEARERS INVOLVED.
WHILE WE DO NOT KNOW WHO BROUGHT THIS ABOUT, OR WHY...
THE FACT REMAINS THAT THE STAGE IS NOW THEIRS.
SHOULD SOMETHING HAPPEN AF-TERWARDS, THEN, AND ONLY THEN...
WILL IT BE OUR TURN TO ACT.

WAP
SKSHHHH
SKSHHHH
GRAK

SNAP
....
GRISH
NGH !!!
SKSHHHHHH
WSHHH

KLATTER
SEMPAI ...!!!
WAP
TCH.
AH, DRAT!
KLANK

JUST WHERE...
!!
FWOOM
SHOVE
DO YOU THINK YOU'RE GOING?!!
WHOK
NN...
OOF !!
RNG
RNG
RNG
......

PAY TOO MUCH ATTENTION TO YOUR SISTER-IN-ARMS AND YOU WILL WIND UP LOSING YOUR *OWN STAR.*
RGH!
HAAAAAH !!!
WHISH
TAKE MY STAR AND YOU CAN MOVE TO DEFEND YOUR HEAVEN SWORD.
HOWEVER, WHILE YOU CONCENTRATE ON THAT, YOUR PARTNER REMAINS IN DANGER, MAKING YOU WORRY.
KRAK
KRAK
KRAK
!!
BUT SHOULD I DO SOMETHING LIKE, SAY...
QUITE AMUSING, I THINK.

WHUMP
THIS --!
THOK
UNF ...!!
KOFF
IT BECOMES EVEN MORE ENTER-TAINING.
I HAVEN'T STOLEN YOUR STAR...
BUT YOU CAN'T STEAL MINE.
NOR CAN YOU DO ANYTHING TO DEFEND YOUR HEAVEN SWORD. ALL YOU CAN DO IS WATCH.
YOU MUST BE FRUS-TRATED!!

WHAT?
YOU WANT ME TO PICK IT UP?
SHF
......
AAH, NOT TOO HAPPY, ARE YOU?
YOU'VE ONLY BEEN ABLE TO HURT ME IN ONE PLACE SO FAR, AFTER ALL.
OR ARE YOU HOLDING BACK FROM ATTACKING AN UNARMED OPPONENT...
OUT OF SOME TEENY VESTIGE OF SWORDS-MANSHIP?
HNNNGH
NN ...!
SEMPAI !!
SEMPAI, ENOUGH! DON'T TRY TO STAND!!
IT DOESN'T MATTER WHAT HAPPENS NOW, YOU'RE HURT BADLY ENOUGH THAT THE JUDGES WILL HALT THE MATCH!!
....
YUKA-RI...
TOTTER

WHAT HAP-PENED TO YOU?
YOU'RE IN AN AWFULLY INTER-ESTING POSI-TION...
TOTTER TOTTER
WHA ...?!
SEMPAI!! WHAT ARE YOU TALKING ABOUT?! NOW IS NOT THE TIME FOR THAT!!
GOOD. IF YOU'RE THAT EN-ERGETIC, YOU SHOULD BE FINE.
...!
YUKARI.
YOU MADE ME A PROMISE, REMEM-BER?
I MEAN, YOU CAN GET OUT OF THAT HOLD, RIGHT?
SHF
FWISHH
YOU SAID YOU WOULD PROTECT ME.

……
DWUH?!
THE HELL?!!
STUPID KIJI!! GO OVER-BOARD WITH THE SMOKE JUST A LITTLE?!
HOW'S SHE EXPECT US TO FIND ANYBODY IN THIS SOUP?!
AUGH!!
Whoaaa…
fwoooo
FWISH
OI…
DON'T TELL ME ALL THIS IS…?
HHH
Y'know. THAT.
OH, UH, YEAH.
IT IS. THAT LOSER KIJI DID HER THING.
KUGA-SAN'S PLAN WAS TO HAVE HER FILL THE WHOLE RANK A AREA TO THE TIPPY TOP WITH FOG SO'S WE COULD SNEAK IN WITHOUT ANYBODY SPOTTING US.
RIGHT. GOT IT.
JUN GETS THE *SPECIAL* THRASHING MENU THIS TIME.
Wanko's givin' her a hand, too.
Isn't this so cool?!
They're workin' together on it.
Swinging for the fences.
HUH?
BRR! DID SOMEONE JUST STEP ON MY GRAVE?
FREEZE
God!
DON'T TELL ME YOU'RE FEELING SICK TODAY, TOO!
MENU

Hn?
OH, NO NO.
IT'S JUST, WE'RE IN THE MIDDLE OF THE HOSHI-TORI AND ALL, SO THERE'S A LOT OF CHARGED ENERGY FLOWING AROUND...
I'm fine, I'm fine.
I GUESS SO...
AND IT SEEMS LIKE MY FRIENDS ARE DOIN' THEIR BEST OUT THERE.
That might be why.
HEH. WELL, I'M UP IN THE CHEERING SECTION TODAY...
SO WHY DON'T I JUST SEND THEM SOME POSITIVE "DON'T GIVE UP!" THOUGHT-WAVES BACK.
Aah...
SO YOU SWORD BEARERS CAN READ PEOPLES ENERGY AND STUFF, HUH?
....
BY THE WAY...
OUR CLASS WAS SUP-POSED TO BE A FESTIVE MAID CAFE.
WHAT HAPPENED TO ALL THE FESTIVE PARTS I WORKED SO HARD ON?
OH, SO YOU FINALLY NOTICED? THEY GOT CENSORED AND RE-MOVED.
First thing in the morning, Day 1.
HONESTLY, THAT "SEXY SHOOTING GALLERY" AND THOSE ADULT CANDY PUZ-ZLES WERE NEVER GOING TO GET PAST REGULATIONS IN THE FIRST PLACE.
HAVING TO RE-DECORATE THE WHOLE CLASSROOM FIRST THING IN THE MORNING WAS A TOTAL PAIN IN THE BUTT, TOO!!
YEAH! NOW YOU GET TO MAKE UP FOR THAT! GET TO WORK!!
RIGHT, RIGHT. SORRY! I'M GOING!
Hey, I made all your outfits, remember...?
TMP

WHAT'S ALL THE RUSH FOR ALL OF A SUDDEN, MUDOU-SAN?
IS SOME-THING WRONG?! DID YOUR PANTIES RIP WHEN YOU CLIMBED OVER THAT WALL?!
Is it all hanging out, now?
DMP
DMP
DMP
NO THEY DID NOT, YOU GUTTER-BRAINED MINI-PERV!!
YOU AND JUN DIDN'T THINK ABOUT A THING WHEN YOU SET ALL THIS UP, DID YOU?!
WITH THIS MUCH FOG, EVEN THE JUDGES WON'T BE ABLE TO SEE ANYTHING!
THEY'RE GOING UP AGAINST A DANGEROUS OPPONENT, AND YOU ALL NIXED THE ONLY OUTSIDE CONTROL ON THE FIGHT!
SO NOW THERE'S NOBODY THERE TO PUT ON THE BRAKES IF IT GETS OUT OF HAND!
THAT MEANS WHAT WAS A RISKY MATCH IN THE FIRST PLACE, JUST HAD ITS DANGER-LEVEL KICKED OFF THE CHARTS!

EVERY-THING'LL BE OKAY IF THE JUDGES SOMEHOW FOUND THEM AND HAVE A HANDLE ON THINGS.
BUT IF THEY HAVEN'T, WE NEED TO FIND THEM *FAST.*
BECAUSE I KNOW *THOSE* TWO, AND THEY SURE AS HELL WON'T FIGHT FAIR!
OH, DEAR. THAT SOUNDS TERRI-BLE.
TP TP TP TP TP TP
SO WHO IS IT YOU ARE LOOKING FOR?
WAUGH?!!

WHITE UNI-FORM!!!
WHI-
OKAY, EVERYONE, STOP RIGHT THERE.
SHF
YOU CAN'T BE IN HERE.
SCREEEE
ANYONE RANK B OR LOWER ISN'T ALLOWED TO ENTER THIS AREA.
IF YOU CAME IN HERE *KNOWING* THAT, I'M GOING TO HAVE TO REPORT YOU.
URK.
I'M NOT SAYING I WON'T LISTEN IF YOU HAVE A REASON TO BE HERE, YOU KNOW.
THERE'S ONLY ONE MATCH CURRENTLY UNDERWAY IN HERE. ARE YOU LOOKING FOR EITHER OF THOSE PAIRS?
YES, MA'AM. WE'RE SORRY.
IT'S JUST WE'RE REALLY CONCERNED A FRIEND OF OURS MIGHT'VE GOTTEN IN OVER HER HEAD.
YEAH!! WE GOTTA GO HURRY AND CHEER HER ON OR ELSE SHE COULD BE IN TROUBLE!!
YUKARI AND HER ATTENDANT ARE IN A REALLY BIG, TOUGH FIGHT AND WE GOTTA GO HELP HER!!
HER WHA ...?!
HER NAME'S "MAKI-SAN," PIP-SQUEAK!! **DON'T BE RUDE!!!**
She's not any-body's "atten-dant"!!!
QUAAAACK!!
O-OH REALLY?
WE WERE JUST LOOKIN' FOR THE OKONOMIYAKI STAND! GUESS WE GOT A LITTLE LOST...
RIIIGHT.
I SEE YOU TWO ARE OBVI-OUSLY LYING.
Right?
Yeah! That's what we were doing!

Wait...
MAKI?
AS IN "KAMIJOU MAKI"?
High school, first year, right?
HN?
OH, UH, YES, MA'AM. SHE'S MY FRIEND'S SISTER-IN-ARMS.
OH REALLY...
SO SHE'S COME BACK TO THE HOSHITORI...
She's always so quiet...
SO YOU'RE SAYING...
KAMIJOU'S FIGHTING THE JU/HIMURO PAIR.
TAP
TAP
OKAY, EVERYONE!
THANK YOU FOR BEING SO COOPERATIVE! NOW PLEASE LEAVE THE RANK A AREA IMMEDIATELY!
CLAP
Just follow me.
HUH?
DOOOOM
WH-WHA?! WE DIDN'T EVEN GET TO SEE THE FIRST HAIR ON YUKARI'S HEAD!!
I SEE...
E-EXCUSE ME...!
IF WE HAVE TO LEAVE, CAN YOU AT LEAST MAKE SURE THERE ARE JUDGES PRESENT, FIRST?
DON'T WORRY.
I'VE ALREADY REPORTED THEIR EXACT LOCATION TO THE JUDGES.
I EXPECT THEY HAVE AT LEAST ONE JUDGE ON SITE ALREADY.
THEIR BATTLE WILL BE CONDUCTED COMPLETELY WITHIN THE RULES.

......
OH...
DON'T LOOK SO CREST-FALLEN. YOU'RE MAKING ME FEEL LIKE THE BAD GUY.
THE RULES OF THE HOSHITORI REQUIRE BATTLES TO BE ON EQUAL GROUNDS FOR ALL SWORD BEARERS.
I WON'T REPORT YOU FOR HAVING BEEN IN HERE...
BUT I AM GOING TO ASK YOU TO LEAVE AND WAIT OUTSIDE THE GATES.
WHEW!!
Saved by the skin of our butts!
....
BESIDES, NOW THAT I'VE SPOTTED YOU, I CAN'T PRETEND THAT I HAVEN'T. NOT IN GOOD CON-SCIENCE.
YES, MA'AM.
WE UNDER-STAND.
So what's gonna happen to us, now?
They're going to string us up for sure!
GIVEN THE OPPONENT, I CAN UN-DERSTAND WHY YOU WOULD BE CON-CERNED.
Sigh
BUT DON'T WORRY.
IF YOUR FRIEND'S PARTNER IS THE PERSON I'M THINKING SHE IS...
THEN YOUR WORRY MIGHT ACTUALLY BE MIS-PLACED.

GOOOOOONG
THERE'S THE BELL.
ONLY THREE MINUTES LEFT.
MY RIGHT WRIST IS COM-PLETELY USELESS.
NO GETTING BY WITH MY PREVIOUS FORM, THEN.
AH WELL, THAT NOTWITH-STANDING...

WAP
DAMN IT ALL.
I'M SURPRISED WE HAVEN'T BEEN STOPPED BY THE JUDGES YET. THAT'S A PRETTY LUCKY BREAK...
FOR US.
SWF
...

......
FWSH
KRAK
KRAK
KRAK
KRAK
KRAK
WOOSH
WHRL
THWAK
!

…
FSH
SKSH
SKSHHH
…
HMM, YEAH. A LITTLE TOUGHER THAN I'D HOPED.
THIS SWORD WASN'T EXACTLY DESIGNED FOR THAT STYLE.
FWSH
!
Tch!
SEM-PAI…
HEH. NOT ONE OF MY STRONGER POINTS, IS IT?
IF I WANTED TO USE THIS TO FINALLY PUT EVERYTHING TO REST…
I SHOULD HAVE GONE AHEAD AND HAD MY SWORD CHANGED AHEAD OF TIME!
YUKARI…

I GIVE THIS STAR TO YOU.
!
I'VE FOUND THEM!
RANK A AREA, MATCH STILL IN PROG-RESS!
RSTL
......
AH!!
Hnf!
LET...
GO!!
!
YUKARI!
IF I CAN STEAL THIS STAR...

SEMPAI!!!
I'LL BE THERE IN JUST A FEW SECONDS!!
PLEASE TRY TO *HANG ON* UNTIL THEN!!!

......

HEH.
THAT'S RIGHT.

BY TAKING THIS STAR...

I CAN SAVE YOU.

I'LL BE WAITING RIGHT HERE.
YUKARI!

AH, PUTTING ON A BRAVE FRONT, ARE WE?
I LIKE THAT.
IT MAKES IT THAT MUCH MORE AMUSING WHEN I CRUSH YOU!!
AND THE NEXT STAR I STEAL WILL BE FOR YOUR PRECIOUS FRIEND.

LEADER!
KAMIJOU/ SOMEYA PAIR'S HEAVEN SWORD IS OBVIOUSLY INJURED.
SHOULDN'T WE HALT THE MATCH?
....
Um...

NO. LET THEM CONTINUE.
I HAVE THE FEELING THAT, IF WE TRIED TO STOP THEM NOW, WE'D GET OURSELVES KILLED.
....

IF I CAN MAKE IT THAT FAR... THEN... I THINK...

I'LL FINALLY FIND THE SKY I'VE BEEN LOOKING FOR.

KAMIJOU-SAN'S MOTHER WON THAT TITLE THREE YEARS IN A ROW.

AND IT SEEMS KAMIJOU-SAN HAS INHERITED HER MOTHER'S TALENT IN FULL.
THOUGH, BEING STUCK WITH A KATANA THROUGH RANK B DIDN'T REALLY ALLOW HER TO EXERCISE THAT TALENT MUCH.
The two blade styles are completely different, right down to their stances.
REALLY ...?

Yep!
IT ISN'T SURPRISING THAT YOU DIDN'T KNOW.
AH! Intruders...!
I MEAN, EVEN I HAVE ONLY SEEN KAMIJOU-SAN'S ORIGINAL FORM JUST ONCE.

IT WAS DURING THE SCHOOL FESTIVAL THE YEAR BEFORE YOU ENROLLED HERE.
THE FENCING CLUB PUT ON A DEMONSTRATION, AND SHE PARTICIPATED.
HER SKILL WAS ELEGANT AND BEAUTIFULLY PRECISE.
AFTER WATCHING A PERFORMANCE LIKE THAT, YOU COULDN'T HELP BUT REMEMBER HER NAME.
WHOA!!
THAT'S SO COOL!!!
I DIDN'T KNOW SEMPAI-SAN WAS SECRETLY THAT AWESOME!!
HOOOO!!...
THAT'S LIKE FINDING OUT THE CHEAPO BOX-CUTTER YOU GOT OUT OF THE 100-YEN BIN REALLY HAD A SOLINGEN BLADE IN IT!!
......
I HAVE NO IDEA WHAT YOU'RE TRYING TO SAY, BUT SHUT UP ANYWAY.
Knowing you, it's rude and stupid.
Or! Or! Or you get what you think is a panda, but it's really a chau chau!!
Like that! Y'know?!
BTHMP
BTHMP
BTHMP

ANYWAY, WITH THAT BEING THE CASE...
I DON'T THINK THAT YOU HAVE AS MUCH TO WORRY ABOUT AS YOU THINK.
I WOULD SAY, GIVEN THE CHANCE TO CONCENTRATE TOTALLY ON STEALING THE OTHER HEAVEN'S STAR, KAMIJOU-SAN HAS THE GREATER SKILL.
OH! OR IS IT YOUR FRIEND YOU ARE MORE CONCERNED ABOUT?
IS SHE NOT CAPABLE?
N-NO, MA'AM ...!
SOMEYA-SAN IS STRONG.
REALLY STRONG.
OH, GOOD. THEN IT ALL SHOULD BE FINE.
I'M SURE BY NOW THEY'VE MANAGED TO TAKE THE OTHER PAIR'S STAR.
EVEN IF THEY HAVEN'T, THERE'S ONLY TWO MINUTES OR SO LEFT.
EVERY-THING WILL BE DECIDED THEN.

PART OF CHEERING SOMEONE ON IS TO BELIEVE IN THEM.
SO WHY DON'T YOU JUST HANG BACK, WAIT, AND HAVE FAITH?
KRAK
KRAK
KRAK
KRAK
WIN...
KRAK
KRAK
KRAK
KRAK
KRAK
KRAK
HAVE TO WIN...!
I'M SURE THAT BEFORE TOO LONG...
YOU'LL SEE THEM COME STUMBLING BACK, ARMS AROUND EACH OTHER'S SHOULDERS WITH SMILES ON THEIR FACES.
#36 END

NEXT U
BENIBAC

JUST KIDDING
IT'LL BE
TSUKISHIMA,
HOSHIKAWA.

POSTSCRIPT

AND HERE'S VOLUME 6———!! THIS ALSO MARKS THE BEGINNING OF *HAYATE X BLADE'S* FOURTH YEAR OF SERIALIZATION. EVERY DAY, I DRAW THIS MANGA AND WONDER WHICH WILL COME TO AN END FIRST—THE BRIGHT FLAME OF LIFE THAT BURNS WITHIN ME, OR THE BONFIRE OF LIFE THAT BURNS WITHIN THIS MANGA?
ANYWAY, ON A MORE SERIOUS NOTE, I'M STARTING TO FORM A HEALTHY DISLIKE OF DRAWING MAID OUTFITS. (WHO'S IDEA WAS IT TO START? MINE...) THE SCHOOL FESTIVAL ARC ONLY HAS ANOTHER TWO CHAPTERS OR SO REMAINING IN THE NEXT VOLUME, SO IF YOU COULD HANG IN THERE AND STICK AROUND FOR THE LAST LITTLE BIT, I WILL BE TRULY GRATEFUL. MY APOLOGIES FOR DRAGGING IT OUT SO LONG.
OH, ON A TOTALLY DIFFERENT SUBJECT, I TRIED DRAWING A VARIANT COVER FOR THIS VOLUME! WELL, OKAY, SO I BEGGED AND THEY EVENTUALLY LET ME DRAW A VARIANT COVER. AND YET AGAIN, I START SOMETHING I EVENTUALLY WISH I HADN'T, BECAUSE, WOW, I'M TIRED... REALLY, REALLY TIRED... ANYWAYS, THE VARIANT COVER WAS ONLY EVER PRINTED IN VERY SMALL NUMBERS, SO UNFORTUNATELY, MANY OF YOU MAY NOT GET TO SEE IT. BUT FOR THOSE WHO DO, I HOPE YOU ENJOY IT. SEE YOU ALL NEXT VOLUME~!!

✿ 林家 2007. 1 ✿
HAYASHIYA

✿ FOREVER MY SUPER HEROINE AND SAVING GRACE, REN MAKISE ✿ TANKYU!

✿ AND A GREAT BIG THANK YOU TO EDITOR NARI-SHI'S FRIEND'S ROOMMATE FOR THE HELP WITH ENSOO'S CHINESE! THANK YOU SO MUCH!

HONORIFICS GUIDE

To ensure that all character relationships appear as they were originally intended, all character names have been kept in their original Japanese name order with family name first and given name second. For copyright reasons, creator names appear in standard English name order.

In addition to preserving the original Japanese name order, Seven Seas is committed to ensuring that honorifics—polite speech that indicates a person's status or relationship towards another individual—are retained within this book. Politeness is an integral facet of Japanese culture, and we believe that maintaining honorifics in our translations helps bring out the same character nuances as seen in the original work.

The following are some of the more common honorifics you may come across while reading this and other books:

-san – The most common of all honorifics, it is an all-purpose suffix that can be used in any situation where politeness is expected. Generally seen as the equivalent to Mr., Miss, Ms., Mrs., etc.

-sama – This suffix is one level higher than "-san" and is used to confer great respect upon an individual.

-kun – This suffix is commonly used at the end of boys' names to express either familiarity or endearment. It can also be used when addressing someone younger than oneself or of a lower status.

-chan – Another common honorific. This suffix is mainly used to express endearment towards girls, but can also be used when referring to little boys or even pets. Couples are also known to use the term between one another to convey a sense of cuteness and intimacy.

Sempai – This title is used towards one's senior or "superior" in a particular group or organization. "Sempai" is most often used in a school setting, where underclassmen refer to upperclassmen as "sempai," though it is also commonly said by employees when addressing fellow employees who hold seniority in the workplace.

Sensei – Literally meaning "one who has come before," this title is used for teachers, doctors, or masters of any profession or art.

Oniisan – This title literally means “big brother.” First and foremost, it is used by younger siblings towards older male siblings. It can be used by itself or attached to a person’s name as a suffix (*niisan*). It is often used by a younger person toward an older person unrelated by blood, but as a sign of respect. Other forms include the informal “oniichan” and the more respectful “oniisama.”

Oneesan – This title is the opposite of “oniisan” and means “big sister.” Other forms include the informal “oneechan” and the more respectful “oneesama.”

TRANSLATION NOTES

7.5
Akihabara – The Akihabara district of Tokyo, especially the Denki Town area, is well known for having lots of anime- and manga-related stores, including maid cafes.

9.4
Shabu-shabu – A Japanese version of hot-pot dishes. Everyone gathers around a pot of boiling broth and dips thin slices of meat and vegetables in it until cooked. White rice and special dipping sauces are traditionally served alongside it as well.

17.2
Meganee-chan – A compound pun combining “Megane,” the word for “glasses,” and “neechan,” the word for “big sister.”

30.1
Dono – An archaic honorific like Sir or Mistress that would be seen on a formal challenge to a duel.

36.4
Okami – Literally “lady general,” *okami* is the term of address used for a hostess or proprietress.

50.6
Northern Sake Court – In the seventh century, the Japanese Imperial court put resources into the study of brewing and fermentation, and as a result produced excellent *chotei* sake. Mizuchi is still smarting about being called an *okami* and is implying, as a proprietress of a drinking establishment, she would go to the “sake court” to get sake for her place. This is a seriously obscure reference.

98.1

Onigashima – Ogre Island is the name of the land of ogres from the famous Japanese fairy tale *Momotaro.* Here Riona is using it as the pair's stage name. "*Tamakochi-ga-oni*" is her personal stage name.

121.5

In the original Japanese, Hayate botches a well-known old proverb: *"Hara ga hette wa ikusa ga dekinu."*—You can't fight on an empty stomach. Instead of that, Hayate blurts out, *"Hara ga hette wa Ikushima Hiroshi,"* or "Empty stomachs are like Ikushima Hiroshi." Ikushima Hiroshi is a well-known journalist and television show host.

151.5

Wan-wan – Another nickname for Isuzu that plays off of the *"Inu"* (dog) in her last name. *"Wan-wan"* translates as "Woof-woof."

Omake Page

Fundoshi – Are loincloths used as men's underwear, commonly worn before World War II. Nowadays, *fundoshi* are generally worn only when men participate in festival traditions, usually along with a short *happi* coat and headband. However, in 2008, some Japanese companies began selling women's *fundoshi* for everyday use.

THIS IS THE VOLUME IN WHICH YOU SHOCK THE WORLD WITH THE STUNNING FIGURE YOU CUT IN A *LOINCLOTH!*

WHO WOULD *NOT* BE EXCITED?

NO ONE IS GOING TO BE SHOCKED, KAICHO. I'M NOT WEARING A *FUNDOSHI.*

Please stop it with the sparkles...

And shameless lies, already.

NOW, THERE IS A LOT OF PAPERWORK THAT NEEDS TO BE FINISHED BEFORE THE FESTIVAL STARTS, SO WOULD YOU GET TO WORK?

HAYATE CROSS BLADE 6

HAYATE CROSS BLADE
SHIZURU HAYASHIYA

THE END

YOU'RE READING THE WRONG WAY

This is the last page of
Hayate X Blade Volume 6

This book reads from right to left, Japanese style. To read from the beginning, flip the book over to the other side, start with the top right panel, and take it from there.

If this is your first time reading manga, just follow the diagram. It may seem backwards at first, but you'll get used to it! Have fun!